Math Phobia

Strategies to Overcome Apathy

and Improve Performance

Dr. Lourdes Ferrer

Title: Math Phobia

Subtitle: Strategies to Overcome Apathy and Improve Performance

Author: Dr. Lourdes Ferrer

In a time that most high in demand and high-paying degrees require students to have a strong foundation in mathematics – math mediocrity reigns in America! Hating math is culturally acceptable and avoiding math courses is the norm. Math Phobia: Strategies to Overcome Apathy and Improve Performance is the product of three distinct generations, Baby Boomer, Millennial and Z-Generation, working together to provide readers with twelve possible reasons for students' apathy and low performance on standardized tests and twelve strategies that could help schools improve students' attitudes and increase their math proficiency. It is Dr. Ferrer's opinion that math should be a pump and not a filter in the pipeline of student academic success.

ISBN-13:
978-1511802123

ISBN-10:
151180212X

DEDICATION

We dedicate this book to all the students who, in spite of the widespread apathy towards math and low performance on standardized tests, embrace and see the relevance of this magnificent science and have the grit to do whatever it takes to reach proficiency.

Dr. Lourdes Ferrer

SPECIAL THANKS

I want to thank the eighteen students who, in spite of their busy schedules and many academic, extra-curricular and home responsibilities, graciously and with great enthusiasm "jumped" into this research-writing project. They not only participated in the study process but also wrote the eighteen essays that are included in this book. In the fabric of these students' character are the values, beliefs and attitudes that lead to academic and career success. The names of these junior scholars are:

Amairin Dominguez, Arturo Ballines, Ashley McCoy, Breianna Rodriguez, Christian Ramirez, Crystal Magana, Fernanda Valencia, Gerardo Caballero, Gerardo Gonzalez, Jennifer Aguilar, Jennifer Carrillo, Juan Martinez, Juanmanuel Vizcarra, Laura Serna, Lezly Castellanos, Lourdes Serrano, Melany Carrillo and Pablo Meléndez.

I also want to thank the school administrators, teachers and parents who, behind the scenes, provided the assistance and support these junior scholars needed to conduct their research interviews and write their essay papers. I strongly believe that behind every great student, there is an even greater parent or school staff member. I truly appreciate your unsung yet essential support!

Finally, yet importantly, I want to thank the board members and district administration of West Aurora School District 129 for opening the doors that allowed me to facilitate the *Grooming for Excellence Student Leadership Academy,* an academic program that permitted and empowered these junior scholars to participate in this eye-opening and relevant book project.

CONTENTS

CONTENTS (CONTINUED)

INTRODUCTION

Perhaps after seeing the cover of this book, you are curious about the topic or you are aware and concerned about the widespread apathy towards mathematics and students' low performance in the math portion of state, national and international standardized tests. For whatever reason, thank you!

Hi! I am Dr. Lourdes Ferrer, *National Academic Consultant*, specialized in *Academic Achievement Gaps and Community Outreach.* Never, in my 40-year career in education, have I been so worried about the economic future of our nation. Countries all around the world are realizing that their ability to compete in today's global economy will strongly depend on their ability to provide their children an up-to-date quality education. In a time that most high in demand and high-paying degrees require students to have a strong foundation in mathematics – **math mediocrity reigns in America!** Hating math is culturally acceptable and avoiding math courses is the norm. We are in the midst of a national math crisis that could easily lead to an economic catastrophe. This is heart breaking and totally unacceptable!

I, a baby-boomer, with the collaboration of my daughter Deborah Ferrer, a millennial and eighteen z-generation junior scholars from West Aurora High School, wrote the book, *Math Phobia: Strategies to Overcome Apathy and Improve Performance.* Three distinct generations, with three different perspectives, working together to provide readers like you an opportunity to reflect on twelve possible reasons for students' apathy towards mathematics and low performance and consider twelve strategies that could help schools improve students' attitudes and increase their math proficiency.

We are respectfully asking you to join us in our effort to counteract our nation's math dimness. Mathematics, in my opinion, should be a pump and not a filter in the pipeline of student academic success. I believe in the power of mathematics! It is a godly science with a divine language that cannot be reached through any of our senses. It can only be understood and contemplated through the power of the human mind. Like I always tell my students, "If you do math, you can do anything!"

PROLOGUE

To me, it feels like the world is being transformed right in front of my eyes! Don't you think? If you are a Baby Boomer like me, you will agree that the way we live our lives today is completely different from 30, 20 or even 10 years ago. Few nights ago, during one of my *In the Driver's Seat* seminars, I asked the parents, "Why do you think the world is changing so fast?" Anxious to respond, one of the moms said, "It is technology! Technology is changing the way we live our lives."

We are in the Information Era, also known as the Computer Age. It is a period in human history in which most nations are inter-connected and dependent on each other for economic purposes. As a result, the nations are aggressively seeking worldwide economic leadership and power. More than ever before, nations' leaders are realizing that their ability to compete in today's global economy will strongly depend on their ability to provide their children or future generations, an up to date quality education.

Like anything else, the meaning of a quality education has also evolved. Our students, from Pre-K to 12th grade, are now required to reach levels of education previously unseen in the history of our nation. To guarantee our children's future employability and our nation's ability to compete with the rest of the world, schools in America are implementing academic curriculums far more demanding compared to those from decades ago. Students are now required to master rigorous academic content, at earlier grade levels, and they must do so at a "microwave" rather than "conventional oven" speed.

This is why most (if not all) states across our great nation are implementing the CCS (Common Core Standards) and the PARCC (Partnership for Assessment of Readiness for College and Career). Both the CCS and the PARCC emphasizes understanding of key literacy and mathematics concepts and the application of knowledge to real world situations in order to ensure that students are better prepared for success in college and today's workforce.

Our government officials and educational leaders are specifically and deeply concerned about our children's lack of proficiency or low performance in mathematics. According to the 2011 *TIMSS (Trends of International Math and Science Study)*, a worldwide study that takes place every four years, 4th and 8th grade students from Korea, Hong Kong-CHN, Japan, Chinese Taipei-CHN, the Russian Federation, etc. are outperforming their peers in the United States in Mathematics and Science. Our nation's leaders believe that this is alarming and a cause for great concern. In a high-tech global economy, our students' lack of math and science proficiency can diminish the nation's leadership and financial strength.

For example, only 22% of 8th grade students from the United States were able to get the right answer to the following problem:

> *P and Q represent two fractions on the number line and P × Q = N. Which of these shows the location of N on the number line?*

Fifty-three percent, 47%, 45% and 44% of their peers from Chinese Taipei, Hong Kong-CHI and Singapore chose the alternative D, which is the right answer. This means that 78% of our 8th grade students could not see or did not know that if P and Q represent two fractions that are less than one, then the product of them has to be less than each one of them. In other words-

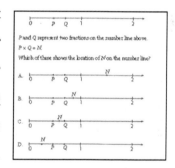

If $p = \frac{1}{2}$ and $Q = \frac{1}{3}$, then $\frac{1}{2} x \frac{1}{3} = \frac{1}{6}$, which is less than ½ and less than ⅓.

Nationally, our students are also performing very poorly in math. According to the *NAEP (National Assessment of Educational Progress)*, only 35% of 8th grade students demonstrated proficiency in the math portion of this national test, which means that 65% of them are performing below grade level in math.

For example, only 16% of 8th grade students knew how to calculate the percent of increase from 50 to 60 cents. The answer is 20% (Choice B) because the difference between 50 and 60 is 10, and 10 out of 50 is .20 or 20%. It troubles me that 84% of our 8th grade students did

> If the price of a can of beans is raised from 50 cents to 60 cents, what is the percent increase in the price?
> A. 83.3%
> B. 20%
> C. 18.2%
> D. 16.7%
> E. 10%

not know how to solve a simple 2-step percent problem.

More concerning is the significant and stubborn academic achievement gaps that continue to exist between ethnic groups in the United States. These inequalities are more evident in mathematics. White and Asian students outperform their Hispanic and African American peers, the two largest minorities, in all the 50 states. In 2013, for example, only 21% and 14% of Hispanics and Blacks passed the math portion of the NAEP, compared to 45% and 60% of Whites and Asians – an alarming performance gap of 46 points between Asians and Blacks.

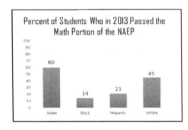

Percent of Students Who in 2013 Passed the Math Portion of the NAEP

African American and Hispanic students together represent a large segment of the America's K-12 student population. With their sheer numbers alone, the level of academic achievement that these two ethnic groups achieve will greatly determine the economic future of our nation.

According to the *ACT Profile National Graduating Class 2013* report, many of our students are graduating high school not ready for a college-level course work. Only 44% of the 2013 graduating class met the math ACT Readiness Benchmark of 22. We must keep in mind that the ACT is the assessment that most higher education institutions use to determine who meets the criteria to pursue in high-in-demand degrees; is eligible to take college-level courses, instead of prep; and, entitled to receive grant and scholarship money. In other words, the scores that students earn in a test like this will have an immediate and long-term impact in the students' academic lives.

Educational leaders are very concerned about the consistent and major performance gaps that also exist between ethnic groups in this high stake test. According to this same report (*ACT Profile National Graduating Class 2013*), 75% of Asians and 53% of Whites passed the math portion of this

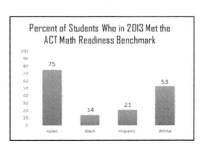

test compared to 14% of Blacks and 30% of Hispanics. This means that 86% of Blacks and 70% of Hispanics are not proficient in mathematics. It is also disturbing the huge performance gap of 61 points between Asians and Blacks. This lack of math proficiency has had, and continues to have, a significant negative impact in the lives of many students, especially Hispanics and African Americans.

First, students who do not meet the ACT math benchmark score are required to spend precious time, money and energy taking prep courses, classes that do not count towards their college education. For example, in most colleges, students must earn at least a 22 ACT math score to take *College Algebra* or *College Statistics*.

Second, colleges are reporting that a significant number of students who end up in these remedial courses never graduate. In a college remedial or prep class, students are required to learn, in three hours per week during a semester, what they could had learned in five hours per week during a year. Many of them find this too hard to achieve, give up and drop out of college. Not long ago, a freshman college student who was taking remedial math said to me,

> *"Now that I am older and busier, I have to learn what I should had learned when I was in high school. I have less time to learn and less support from the teachers. I am not sure if I can do this!"*

Third, the lack of math proficiency also prevents students from pursuing degrees that lead to high in demand and high-paying jobs. Since 84% and 70% of African American and Hispanic students do not pass the math portion of the ACT, they are more likely to pursue degrees that are not in demand, which leads to unemployment or under-employment.

I have been a mathematics teacher for many years, at the high school and graduate school levels. On a voluntary basis, every year I provide workshops to improve students' performance on the ACT. In these past weeks alone, I have explained how to solve 240 ACT math  problems. I know that some of those problems can be challenging. However, many of them only require basic math, careful reading and common sense. When you see the following problems, it could make you scratch your head and say, "What were they thinking when they could not get the right answer?

1. *How many times would you cut a 24-inch ribbon to get three 8-inch pieces? Although* $24 \div 8 = 3$, *the answer is 2 times. To get 3 pieces, you only cut the ribbon twice.*

2. *How many pages does a person read from page 10 through 20? Although* $20 - 10 = 10$, *the answer is not 10 but 11. The word "through" implies that you must include page 20.*

3. *How many cubic feet of dirt is in a hole that is 4ft by 10ft by 6ft? Although the volume of the hole is,* $4 \times 10 \times 6 = 240$, *the answer is not 240 but 0. The word "hole" means that is empty; therefore, there is no dirt!*

As I stated before, most of the college degrees that are in demand in our current economy require students to have a

strong foundation in mathematics. According to Dan Berman, Contributing Editor of ThinkAdvisor, "Engineering and science occupations continued their stranglehold on the top third of the rankings." They found that the top best-paying college majors were *Petroleum Engineering, Chemical Engineering, Nuclear Engineering, Computer Engineering* and *Electrical Engineering.* There is no way a student can successfully pursue any of these degrees without successfully passing a series of rigorous math courses.

Dan Barman also reported that the five degrees currently paying the least are *Child and Family Studies, Elementary Education, Exercise Science, Broadcast Journalism* and *Social Work.* Students who are not competent in mathematics are more likely to pursue degrees like these because they do not require students to take rigorous math courses.

According to researchers at *Princeton-based Educational Testing Service (ETS),* in a test called the *PIAAC (Program for the International Assessment of Adult Competencies),* American Millennials, or people born in the early 1980s in the U.S., fell short when it came to the skills employers want the most –

literacy, practical math and problem-solving. In shock, they reported that, "In numeracy, meaning the ability to apply basic math to everyday situations, Gen Xers [Millennials] in the U.S. ranked dead last." Even the best educated were outperformed by their counterparts in Japan, South Korea, Belgium, etc. They also reported that Millennials, in the 90th percentile, scored lower than their counterparts did in 15 countries and only outperformed their equals from Spain. They considered this alarming!

Madeline Goodman, an ETS researcher who worked in this study, stated that, "We really thought [U.S.] Millennials would do better than the general adult population, either compared to older coworkers in the U.S. or to the same age group in other countries; but they didn't. In fact, their scores were abysmal."

People who are aware of our Millennials inability to solve math problems are troubled by the fact that they could not solve problems that only required basic math

APPLY FOR A LOAN
UP TO 70,000

TERMS OF THE LOAN
PAY ONLY $103 PER MONTH
FOR EACH $1000 BORROWED

understanding applied to real-life situations. For example, many American college-graduates could not answer correctly the following question.

What is the annual rate of simple interest for a loan that the lender charges 103 dollars a month for 12 month for every 1000 dollars that is lend?

The terms of this loan requires people to pay $103 a month for every $1000 they borrow. If that is the case, in 12 months, they would have paid a total amount of $1,236 (103 × 12 = 1236); and, $1236 is $236 more than $1000 (the amount borrowed). Therefore, the question is, "What percent of 1000 is 236?" The answer is- 236 ÷ 1000 = .236 *and .236 equals* 23.6%.

In 1983, the *National Commission on Excellence in Education* issued a report that assessed the quality of education in the U.S. Authors of the report declared that the state of America's education made it "a nation at risk." They concluded that, "What was unimaginable a generation ago has begun to occur—others are matching and surpassing our educational attainments. It is impossible not to see this statement as prophetic!" It appears that, in spite of the many national (and state) school reform initiatives, American students' performance in mathematics is decreasing instead of improving.

As you can see, we are definitely in the midst of a national math crisis that could easily lead to an economic catastrophe. American's perceptions regarding mathematics and math-related subjects such as Chemistry, Physics, Engineering, etc. is rapidly deteriorating. Hating mathematics is culturally acceptable and avoiding them is the norm. Concerned about the future employability of our students and our nations' competiveness, I have spent numerous years trying to find out the reasons behind this so widespread apathy and low performance in the math portions of all local, state, national and international standardized tests, including the PARCC, the ACT, the TIMSS and now the PIAAC. What is going on? What is causing this math mediocrity?

In search for answers, I have put enormous amount of hours asking teachers and school administrators,

> *"Why is it that most high school students avoid taking high level math courses, do so poorly in the math portion of each and every standardized test or have negative attitudes towards mathematics?*

I have surfed the web to learn from other researchers, educators and educational leaders their perspectives regarding mathematics and the way is taught and assessed in the United States. I have even spent hundreds of hours solving many of the math problems students failed to get the right answer in these state, national and international standardized tests. Nevertheless, I decided to go a step further. I said to myself, "Why don't I ask Z-Generation students, those born in the late 90s?" At the end, they are the ones who are currently taking math classes and standardized tests.

I was so glad to learn that 17 students from West Aurora High School and a special guest from Oswego High School, schools located in one of the Northwest suburbs in Illinois, graciously accepted my invitation. Their mission was to do online research and interview their classmates, teachers and parents to learn, from their perspectives:

   a. What are the possible reasons behind students' apathy towards mathematics and low performance on standardized tests?

   b. What can students, teachers and parents do (or not do) to minimize students' apathy and improve their performance in the math portion of standardized tests?

I also asked each one of them to write an essay about their online research and interview findings and recommendations. It was not easy for them! Some of them were not skillful writers and some admitted struggling with math themselves. In spite of their challenges, they jumped into this project with an enthusiasm that surprised many, including myself.

Likewise, I asked my daughter Deborah Ferrer, who happens to be a Millennial, to join us in our search for answers. She is a college graduate with a unique perspective regarding many of the issues that our nation faces. Her insights and thoughts are embroiled in the content of this book and her graphic design and editing skills made the process much easier. Since I am a Baby Boomer, having a Millennial in the team helped me understand the Z-Generation students better.

In my opinion, the beauty of this study and writing project is that it gave me the opportunity to learn from students, teachers, and parents their perspectives about students' apathy towards math and low performance in standardized tests. They also provided me with ideas on how to help students embrace math and improve their scores on standardized tests. This is what this book, *Math Apathy: Strategies to Overcome Apathy and Improve Performance,* is all about. We want to provide readers the opportunity to:

a. Study and reflect upon what we found are the 12 greatest reasons for students' apathy and low performance

b. Consider the 12 strategies we believe can help students develop a positive attitude towards math and improve their performance in their math classes and any standardized test.

According to Pablo Melendez [co-writer],

"...no one should just sit and wait. It is time for everyone to find a solution. A way to pitch in and help is changing this biased and negative belief regarding math. The point is that, if students are mentally wired to think that they are not good at math, they will stay thinking they are not good enough at math."

It is Pablo's math teacher belief that, "We can change this by stop accepting math intolerance from students. It is wrong to believe that they are incapable of performing well at math." According to Pablo, "Mathematics can often appear arcane, esoteric, unworldly and irrelevant." He stated that it is worth remembering what the 17th-century scientist Galileo Galilei once declared:

"The universe cannot be read until we have learned the language and become familiar with the characters in which it is written, the mathematical language. These letters are triangles, circles and other geometrical figures, without which mean it is humanly impossible to comprehend a single word."

This is why I am humbly asking you to help us counteract our nation's math poorness! We want to increase people's awareness regarding the importance, usefulness and beauty of mathematics and we must definitely improve their performance in their math classes and every state, national and international test they take. Mathematics, in my opinion, should be a pump and not a filter in the pipeline of student academic success.

REASONS FOR APATHY
AND LOW PERFORMANCE

Dr. Lourdes Ferrer

REASON # 1

It is culturally acceptable to "hate" or dislike math.

One of the greatest reasons for students' struggles with math and low performance on standardized tests is the widespread negative attitude towards mathematics. According to the students, teachers and parents who participated in this study, this negative attitude is so rooted in the minds of students that it is now part of the American culture. They dislike math the same way that their parents, grandparents and great grandparents did. Therefore, it is "ok" to hate math.

The students expressed that while their peers accept hating mathematics, embracing them can lead to peer rejection. Excelling in math can perceived as being "nerdy" and that is not "cool." In school, disliking mathematics is the norm and liking them the exception. Not long ago, during break time, I heard one of my groomers (a student enrolled in one of my *Grooming for Excellence* Student Leadership Academies) say to another groomer, "Yes, me too! I also hate math. It is my worst subject." When I heard him say that, I took in apart and asked him, "Why are you saying that? Not only you ace every math class but you are also planning to become an Electrical Engineer." Visibly embarrassed for being caught in a lie, he said to me, "I just want to be like the rest. I guess I am trying too hard to fit in."

I must say that this math-dislike or math-hate is not prevalent in all ethnic groups. Students who immigrate into the United States from some Asian countries, or whose parents were born in Asia, usually have a more positive attitude towards math and math-related subjects. Math does not come naturally easier to them. They simply put much more effort to learn it. My son, who teaches high-level math courses in one of Florida's IB (International Baccalaureate) programs, said to me:

> *"I have never heard a negative comment regarding math in any of my IB math classes. Most of my students' parents are from India. For them, failing math in not an option and the pressure to succeed can be unbearable. It worries me sometimes. During parent-teacher conferences, the question that most parents ask is, 'What else can my child do to earn an A in your class?' They truly believe in working really hard to achieve and they feel proud of the amount of effort they put into learning something."*

According to Lourdes Serrano [co-writer],

> *"They [Asians] prepare for a class before they actually take it and might do it for a different reason. Most of their hard work is done for the sake of honoring their families."*

A 21-year-old person that Lourdes interviewed said, "Asians that come to the United States are not yet fully committed to our culture." Lourdes is convinced that people who come from those countries hold on to their values and beliefs. They pass their appreciation for the academics to the next generations. It is Laura Serna's [co-writer] belief that,

> "Rather than lowering our standards, we should raise them! Our society teaches students that it is ok to perform poorly in math. Students think that it is fine to not try to understand math. Students hate math because it is socially acceptable to feel that way."

It is Laura' belief that the United States cannot compete in a global economy if American students continue to hate math and science. In her own words,

> "We cannot go on being consumers of other countries' ideas and discoveries. We have the opportunity to have our own 'space race,' but with our own new ideas. If we fix this, there is no telling what innovations we will see in the future. The future starts in the classroom; so let us make a better tomorrow for all of us."

Concerned about her peer's negative attitude towards math, Breianna Rodriguez [co-author] said,

> "Math-filled careers pay substantially more than the non-math filled. If our generation continue to believe math is useless, the future will be crowded with uneducated masses. Their torpid and immature attitude and lack of effort in learning math will get them to become homeless."

Dr. Lourdes Ferrer

REASON # 2

Most students embrace a "fixed" mindset instead of a "growth" mindset.

The students and teachers who were interviewed in this study, directly or indirectly, confirmed what many educators believe. One of the greatest reasons for students' apathy towards math and poor performance in on standardized tests is that they attribute academic success to factors beyond their control, meaning that students embrace a "fixed-mindset" instead of a "growth-mindset."

The fixed mindset is based on the assumption that if students have to work hard to learn math concepts and algorithms or solve math problems, then they do not have the ability to excel in mathematics. Students with a fixed mindset feel stuck with whatever intelligence they think they were born with. For them, failure or setbacks in a math class means that they do not have what it takes to pass it successfully. Because math is mostly about solving problems, and problems by definition are challenges, they are likely to avoid taking math in fear of being perceived as not smart. When failing a math test, for example, a student with a fixed mindset is likely to say, "I will not spend my time looking at the problems I missed because I do not have the genes to do well. So why try?

On the other hand, the growth mindset is based on the assumption that intelligence, or the ability to learn, is something that can be cultivated. As Dr. Jeff Howard says, "Smart is not something that you are but something you can become through effective effort." Students with a growth mindset believe that the more they challenge themselves the smarter they can become. They think that failure or setbacks in a math class can be overcome by putting more effort. They know that even people with a very high IQ, including famous mathematicians, had to work extensively to accomplish their academic goals. Students with a growth mindset value learning more than "looking smart." Period! When failing a math test, for example, a student with a growth mindset is likely to say, "I will analyze this test to see why I failed it and learn from each mistake I made. With some extra effort, I will nail the next test and improve my grade."

Christian Ramirez [co-author] testified that it took him a while to recognize that if he wanted to excel in higher levels of math courses, he could no longer depend on his innate ability to learn. His success would no longer depend on who he was but on the amount of effort, he would put into learning. In his own words,

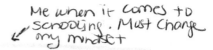

Me when it comes to schooling. Must change my mindset

"*However, honestly, let us be realistic. You master only the material that you practice. I had to get rid of my egotistical mindset that said, 'I'm naturally good at math. I can catch on quickly. That behavior led me to no good; in fact, it brought my GPA down."*

Juanmanuel Vizcarra [co-author] believes that students' mindset regarding math can destroy their motivation to learn and lead them to quit. Students must persist and not give up when they struggle with a math problem. In his own words,

"Solving math problems takes time! Students must understand the process; but if the process does not click right away, they automatically believe that they are not good and stop putting any more effort."

Melany Carrillo [co-author] believes that success in any academic subject is based on students' willingness to persist and grow when confronted with obstacles, instead of accepting defeat. Regarding this she said,

"The students' levity towards math can mostly be blamed on themselves. I believe that if you want to succeed, you will succeed. Like any other goal, academic success will require determination and arduous effort to defeat obstacles and overcome challenges. At the end, this is all about you."

REASON # 3

Students fear ~~how they are perceived them~~ could lead
to rejection.

_M_

One of the leading reasons for students' apathy and low performance in mathematics is their fear of rejection. During interviews, both students and teachers expressed that many students are more concerned about what others think about them than how well they are doing in class. On one hand, if they show too much interest in their math classes, their peers could perceive them as geeks or nerds. On the other hand, if they struggle in class and seek help, their peers or their teachers could judge them as unintelligent. In their minds, being viewed as nerds or intelligent can lead to rejection.

The Oxford Dictionary defines fear as an unpleasant emotion caused by the belief that someone or something is dangerous, likely to cause pain, or a threat. Since adolescents, in particular, have a strong need for acceptance, rejection is an act or feeling that they are likely to fear.

According to Fernanda Valencia [co-writer],

"There are some people who actually like math; but since it is socially acceptable to dislike it, and they want to be like anyone else, they say, 'I hate it too!' People who like mathematics are viewed as nerds in our society and that's not how students want to be viewed. The focus we put on what others think must decrease and the focus that we put on our education should increase."

Students who fear that others might view them as unintelligent usually think that students, who struggle, seek help or ask questions do not have the ability to learn. They hold on to the false assumption that the speed in which students learn defines their level of intelligence. They think that the faster students learn the smarter they are.

Lezly Castellanos [co-author] thinks that not all students learn or comprehend the content taught in class at the same pace; and there is nothing wrong with that. Everyone learns differently. Some may need a little more time, while others catch on quickly. In her own words,

"Students need to ask questions; but nobody does! You may be asking yourself, 'Why is it that no one asks questions if no one understands the lesson?' Well, students are afraid to be perceived by their peers as dumb or stupid for asking questions. They feel like everyone understands the material except for them. This leads to students not learning the material and not performing as well as they should or could."

Through this study, we also found that some students also fear their teachers' rejection. They want their teachers to like them and expressed concern about what their teachers might think or feel about them when they ask questions, seek help or cannot perform as well as others. It was puzzling to see that the students who need help the least are the one who seek help the most. They usually see their teachers as professionals who really care about their education. On the other hand, the students who need help the most are the ones who seek help the least. They think that teachers do not care about the students who struggle in class and will be annoyed if they ask for help. Arturo Ballines [co-author] addressed this fear when he wrote,

> "There are also students who are not assertive enough to ask questions to the teachers. They feel uncomfortable with the teacher or they feel like the teacher will be disappointed for not being able to understand such a simple problem. Sometimes, when students ask the teacher for a little more help, they still end up not understanding the problem. They are afraid to ask the teacher again because some teachers are impatient. This is true!"

Dr. Lourdes Ferrer

REASON # 4

Classroom instruction and climate is not always conducive to learning for all students.

A significant number of the students who participated in this research-writing project stated that some of the reasons behind students' apathy towards math and low performance in class and tests have to do with the quality of classroom of instruction and environment. Among other things, they reported that:

a. Teachers go over the math content too fast;
b. Classroom instruction mostly benefits auditory leaners;
c. Teachers are not able to motivate or engage students; and,
d. Students behave in a disruptive manner.

Amairin Dominguez [co-writer] believes that the math curriculums that teachers must follow are simply too big. She thinks that teachers have too much to teach but not enough time to teach it; so instead of really diving deep into every content that they teach so students can fully understand,

"Teachers graze the surface and move on!" She thinks that most math teachers are rushing all the time and when students see that they cannot catch up, they simply give up! Regarding this, one of the teachers who Amairin interviewed said,

> "When I am teaching, I feel like I don't have a lot of time to really have the students interacting and discovering concepts that might interest them more because of what I am required to get through in a year."

Students think that most math teachers deliver their instruction in a way that benefits auditory and visuals learners, not the kinesthetic/tactual ones. It is Gerardo Caballero's [co-writer] opinion that to decrease apathy towards math and improve performance, math instructors could use a more hands on teaching approach. In his own words,

> "Teachers tend to deliver mathematics in a way that mostly benefits auditory learners. Students with other learning styles shutdown, do not participate, and do not understand. Auditory learners, for example, learn best through the recital of information. Visual learners comprehend information presented to them in the forms of graphics and demonstrations. Kinesthetic learners can better benefit from hands-on methods such as tactual activities and experiments."

If you visit different middle or high school math classes, you will see that most teachers provide their instruction through lectures and visual representations. Students moving around, working with each other, manipulating objects it is harder to see because these types of activities in an algebra, geometry or any math beyond Arithmetic require a significant amount of work including teacher preparation, instructional materials and instructional time. As an experienced math teachers myself, I know that time is a luxury that most teachers do not have.

The students also found that their peers (complaint) about not having quality instructors. They believe that young students need to have a fun and motivating teachers. Arturo Ballines [co-writer] stated that schools should hire better teachers who actually care about their students. He believes that not all teachers love to teach and show their passion for teaching. Ms. Finley, a high school math teacher, said to Arturo,

> "Teachers need to be encouraging. They need to keep everyone interested, engaged in the lesson, and have everyone's eyes up and paying attention. They also need to be better teachers. Teachers need to find easier and better ways to teach."

Students are also reporting that some of their peers are exhibiting behaviors that are disruptive and disrespectful towards their teachers. Interviewed students stated that it is very difficult to pay attention, focus and learn in a math class when students are saying and doing things with the sole purpose of disrupting the class or disrespecting the teacher. One of the students who Laura Serna [co-writer] interviewed said that his math class was a "jungle." When Laura asked why, he explained that his class never respected the teacher and that the teacher spent 99% of class time "babysitting" students instead of teaching.

Students and teachers all agreed that students could learn better, when the classroom climate is conducive to learning. Personally, I was surprised to learn that one of the reasons why 60-plus students attended each of my Saturday morning ACT Math Prep Courses, even in subzero temperatures, was that they were surrounded by other students who also wanted to learn. As one of them said, "I can learn so much better in a crowd like this, even if we hardly fit in the room. Here there is no clowning! Everyone behaves and do what they have to do and that motivates me to do even better."

M

REASON # 5

Parents do not build in their children the mental frame of reference that is conducive to math success.

With certainty, I can say that 100% of the students, teachers and parents who participated in this study stated that students' attitude towards school and their level of academic achievement had a lot to do with their upbringing and home environment. Experts in the field of education agree that one of the leading indicators of student academic success is parent involvement. Regarding the role that parents play in their children's education, one of the teachers who Amairin Dominguez [co-writer] interviewed said,

> "As a teacher, it feels good to get credit for students' high performance; however, it also hurts to take the blame when they fail. Nevertheless, the parents, not the teachers, are the leading contributors of their own children's academic success or failure. How can we expect your children's school to be responsible for their upbringing? Good parenting will result in student success no matter what schools or teachers do."

The mental frame of reference is the lens that we humans use to interpret and react to the world around us. It includes the values, beliefs, attitudes, perceptions and expectations that we learn or acquire from our parents, siblings or people close to us during our upbringing. This means that intentionally (or unintentionally), parents build in their children's lives the same values, beliefs, attitudes, etc. that describes or defines who they are. For example, if parents value education, believe in their children's potential to learn and expect them to achieve, sooner or later, their children will also value education, believe in themselves and expect themselves to achieve.

Years ago, when I was a high school math teacher, I had many students who did not believe they could do well in my class. Previous negative experiences, combined with their parents' low academic expectations killed any hope to excel in math. "You do not understand, Mrs. Ferrer," one parent said to me during a parent-teacher conference; and then he added,

> "José is like a donkey when it comes to mathematics. I was just like him when I was in school. His mom and I are ok if he at least passes your math class so he does not have to take it again next year. Anyways, I appreciate everything you are doing to help him."

There are also parents who do not see the value of exceling in math. They are not aware of the important role that math plays in their children's academic development and the short and long-term negative consequences of lacking math proficiency. There are parents who value extra-curricular activities such as sports or performance arts more than academic subjects such math or science. Throughout the years, I have seen parents express more joy for having their kids excel in sports than excel in math. Sadly, winning a game seems to be more important than acing a rigorous math test. In one of my *In the Driver's Seat* seminars, I asked the parents, "In what way is a 16-lane expressway similar to navigating the American Education System?" With a tone of voice that showed concern, one mom said,

> "If there is some kind of game going on in school, like football or soccer, it is going to be like driving on an expressway during peak time. It is going to be bumper to bumper! However, if it is a math curricular night, where parents learn how to support their children's math education, then it is going to be like driving in the middle of the night. There is no traffic at all."

Most children want their parents to feel proud of them. Therefore, it is very hard for young people to put in the effort needed to excel in math when their parents do not perceive excelling in math as a great success and a reason to be proud. Let us face it. Math is not an easy subject. It requires a lot of work! By experience, I know that students who enroll and do well in courses such as Pre-Calculus, AP Calculus, or AP Statistics, are likely to be the ones whose parents build in their children the mental frame of reference that leads to high levels of math proficiency. These parents not only have a positive attitude towards math and perceive this science as a conduit to academic and career success but also believe in their children's potential to learn and expect them to achieve proficiency.

REASON # 6

Students perceive math as useless.

According to the students who participated in this study, one of the greatest reasons for students' apathy towards math and low performance in the math portion of standardized tests is that they view mathematics as a useless academic subject. They consistently witness students in their math classes asking, "When will I ever use what I am learning in this this class?" Others say,

> *"Why should I work so hard to learn something that has nothing to do with what I am planning to do the rest of my life?"*

Melany Carrillo [co-writer] remembers that when she was a freshmen taking Algebra 1, there was a student sitting in front of her who would constantly fall asleep in class and never paid attention. When he was awake, he would yap that what the teacher was teaching was useless. He would then ask the students around him, "How is this useful in life?" When Melany asked him, "Don't you care about your future?" He confidently said, "When I'm done with high school, I'm going to open a car workshop and be a mechanic! I don't need this."

Concerned about her peers' perceptions regarding math, Crystal Magana [co-writer] said,

> *"I have noticed that many students perceive math as useless. The benefits and beauty of mathematics is practically impossible for many students to see."*

In my long career as an educator, I know that too many students, parents and even some teachers are not aware that math proficiency, among many other things, helps students:

a. Make wiser decisions based on logical thinking rather than emotions;

b. Develop the critical-thinking and problem-solving skills needed to succeed in school and life;

c. Develop discipline by continuously putting effort into solving math problems; and,

d. Build self-confidence and self-esteem by experiencing success after overcoming math challenges.

We also learned that most students do not know that high school graduates, who perform poorly on the math portion of college entrance tests, are usually placed in prep courses; wasting time, money and energy in courses that do not count towards their degree. Because of this, many opt to dropout of college.

I am also concerned by the significant number of high school students who do not know that a weak foundation in mathematics does not allow students to pursue degrees that lead to high in demand and high-paying careers. I have worked with middle and high school students who want to become nurses, medical doctors or physical therapists. Others want to be electrical, chemical or mechanical engineers. All these careers are fantastic! However, when I ask them how well they are doing in math, I get responses such as, "That is my worst subject," "I hate it!" or "I avoid math at all cost." They are not aware that it is impossible to earn a medical, engineering or any STEM-related degree, the ones that are usually in high demand, without successfully passing a series of rigorous math courses.

Juan Martinez [co-writer] thinks that students think they do not need math because no one has never explained to them its importance and usefulness. He believes that students would put more effort into learning math if they knew the positive impact that math proficiency could have in their academic lives and career choices. It is Juan's history teacher's belief that,

> *"Students think that if mathematics is not useful to them, then why bother learning it?"*

Dr. Lourdes Ferrer

REASON # 7

Math is like a "foreign language."

Studying the reasons behind students' apathy towards math and low performance on standardized tests, students found that math, is many ways is like a foreign language. One of the many definitions of language is a system of artificially constructed symbols that allow humans to communicate with each other and preserve ideas. Language acquisition is a process that could easily take years. When students study a foreign language, they must first learn words and then build sentences that clearly communicate ideas. The same is true in mathematics.

In mathematics, many of the words that sound like English might have a different meaning. For example, the word "solution" in chemistry is a homogenous mixture composed of only one phase. In math, the word "solution" is the answer to a problem. For many students mathematics simply does not sound like English.

Mathematics also uses numerous and "strange" symbols to state facts, present ideas or find the solution to a problem.

For example, we use a capital letter to name a set and place its elements into braces (not parenthesis or brackets), separated by commas. A= {1, 2, 3, 4} means, "A is the set of counting numbers less than 5."

In math, terms make up expressions the same way that words make up sentences. The same way that, "I love math" is a sentence with three words, $2x^2$-3x + 2 is a math expression that has three terms. It is very difficult, if not impossible, for students the reach math proficiency or perform well on timed standardized test without mastering the math language.

According to Crystal Magana [co-writer], students have a hard time remembering a language that they only use when they are learning math or solving math problems. Since it is not part of their daily lives, they perceive it as alien or foreign. In her own words,

> *"Math is like a foreign language. It has many symbols, rules and formulas that students must memorize. I have come across people that literally had to cheat their way out of tests. Some would write the formulas in their wrists, on the table, and even on water bottles."*

According to Christian Ramirez [co-writer], students start having problems with math, or see it as a foreign language when they start taking higher levels of math courses. Christian thinks that students are likely to do well in math when they are in grade school. It is in middle and high school, when they take courses like Algebra and Geometry, that they are exposed to variables, symbols and algorithms that appear to be foreign. Regarding this he said,

> "A math problem can be very simple. However, if students see variables, something that they have never seen before, they give up by default. As students take higher-level math courses such as Calculus, they will find math to be more rigorous and problems to be longer and more difficult to solve. It gets to the point where math is a foreign language for too many students."

Dr. Lourdes Ferrer

REASON # 8

Like a sport, math requires intensive practice and hard work.

Most of the students and teachers who participated in this research project expressed that one of the reasons for students' low performance in math is their lack of effort. In other words, students are not practicing or working hard enough to reach math proficiency. Frustrated with his first-semester grade, Carlos, a student who is currently taking Trigonometry said to me,

> *"I go to class every day. I pay attention to the teacher. I even take a lot of notes! In spite of all that, I cannot get anything higher than a C."*

In respond to his comment I said,

> *"Carlos, anything higher than a C in a class like that will require a lot of effort. You do not have any other choice but to harder. "*

I explained to him that going to class and paying attention to the teacher is similar to going to the gym and watching other people play basketball. Students cannot learn how to play basketball by just by watching others play. There are things that we can learn by simply listening or watching. However, other things require practice and hard work. Mathematics is one of them.

Psychologists are reporting that there is a direct statistical relationship between hours of practice and achievement. Practice makes perfection! In the book *Outliers*, Malcolm Gladwell states that practice, more that innate ability, will determine the level of expertise that a person can achieve

Math teachers are consistently stating that the best way for students to practice and increase their math ability is by doing homework - and doing it with integrity! That is the main reason why math teachers give homework. Homework completion is to math proficiency what practice is to a sport championship. Trying to get into the root of Carlos' lack of success, I asked him, "How much time do you spend doing homework?" With a guilty look in his eyes, he said:

> *"Dr. Lourdes, the truth is that I hardly have time to do homework. I have so much stuff to do after school. I have soccer practice almost every day and I also work during weekends."*

A teacher who Amairin Dominguez [co-writer] interviewed, believes that students could have an apathetic attitude towards math because math requires time and does not provide instant gratification. With great conviction she stated,

> "Students have the privilege of looking up anything to get answers at the drop of a hat. Any topic that they want to know or read about, they Google it and thousands of sites pop up for them to click and begin finding answers."

It is this teacher's opinion that math is a class that requires time because students must solve problems, with multiple routes that could possibly lead to dead ends. It involves a lot of hard work. In her own words:

> "I don't believe students really take much time to think of a game plan to reason through problems, and once they get stuck they just give up. Many students do not take the time to sit down and study for their tests; and, if it is not something that comes naturally or easy to them, they have a tendency to just give up."

Frustrated with her peers' lack of willingness to put in the necessary effort to learn mathematics, Breianna Rodriguez [co-author] said,

> "After all, why not suck it up and push through the hardships to perform well in math? Being able to see the accomplished work that was completed with such ambition is usually worth the extensive, tedious and on occasion, repetitive homework. If students were a bit more meticulous with the assignments they turned in, and saw their grades at their optimum, then they would be captivated to transact their best every time. Math can be problematic! It is very easy to fall behind but extremely difficult to catch up. However, nothing worth pursuing can be achieved without pain, mentally or physically."

Dr. Lourdes Ferrer

REASON # 9

Like any other natural science, math requires that students memorize, focus and work meticulously.

The students and teachers who participated in this study agreed that one of the reasons behind students' apathy and low performance in mathematics is their lack of ability to memorize, focus and work meticulously. Math teachers, especially those that have been teaching for more than two decades are reporting that students more than ever before are lacking the ability to memorize math concepts, facts and algorithmic procedures. In my opinion, there are several reasons for this lack of ability to remember.

The first might be that teachers spend most of their instructional helping students develop critical thinking and problem solving skills and allow students to rely on formula sheets, charts and calculators to find the answer to problems that require memorization. At the elementary school grades, for example, students do not memorize the timetables, the definition of basic geometric shapes or the correlation between inches, feet, yards, etc. At the secondary school grades, students do not memorize the formula to change a temperature from Fahrenheit to Celsius, the square root of numbers such as 9, 25 or 144 or the difference between a rational and an irrational number.

Students, teachers and parents are also reporting that technological devices are also diminishing students' need to memorize. Regarding this, Fernanda Valencia [co-writer] said,

> *"In our era, everything can be solved with a GPS, a calculator or with internet access. Since we no longer have the discipline or thrive to solve things for ourselves, it is easy to give up when a problem arises that cannot be solved with an electronic device. Mathematics is a subject that requires time, concentration and memorization."*

Reyna, a student that Fernanda interviewed, said, "It is so much easier to take out my phone and google the formulas. No one wants to think that much." Someone once said, "You will use whatever you do not use." Students do not spend time and effort learning strategies to memorize things because they might not see the need to do so.

Math is also a science and like any other science, it requires that students pay attention and focus. Students today, at all levels, are required to go beyond simple computations and basic mathematical algorithms. Besides knowing by memory concepts, rules, and algorithms, they must use critical thinking and problem-solving skills to find the solution to multi-step math problems, in different contexts or real life situations. These types of math problems require students to concentrate and concentration is all about focus.

The ability to concentrate does not come naturally to many people, including myself. Like anything else, focus is a skill that students sooner, rather than later, must acquire. Students who focus can avoid diversions when sitting in their math classes, doing their homework or studying for a math test. This is extremely difficult, especially for the Z-Generation students. They have to resist continuous temptations to engage in activities such as using their Smart phones, texting a friend, seeing what their friends posted in Instagram or watching a TV reality show.

Lourdes Serrano [co-writer] believes that some parents do not provide their children a home environment in which they can focus in their education. A parent that she interviewed said that studying is not enforced in many students' homes because their homes are "bombarded" with all kinds of distractions to the point that students cannot concentrate in their schoolwork. Lourdes also stated that some students could not focus in their education because they have too many home responsibilities like cooking, taking care of their younger siblings or running errands for their parents.

Although math is a natural science, it is different from all of them in the way evidence is collected and ideas are tested. Math is mostly an abstract science. It cannot be perceived through any of the five human senses. For example, you can see microorganisms (Biology), feel temperature (physics), or smell substances (chemistry). However, never in life, you will see, smell, taste, hear or touch $\sqrt{2}$ (the square root of two) or $a^2 + b^2 = c^2$ (the Pythagorean Theorem). Math can only be studied or communicated through symbols perfectly arranged or put together to represent concepts, ideas or algorithms. That is why solving math problems require students to not only memorize and focus but also to be extremely meticulous.

There are many ways to solve a problem but only one answer. Any little mistake a student make can lead him or her to the wrong answer. In a one-to-one conversation that I had with a student who failed her semester test due to careless mistakes, she said to me,

> *"I knew the content! I just failed the test because of the stupid mistakes I made. I guess there is too much going on in my life. It is hard for me to concentrate. I know how to do the problems. I just do not see the details."*

We are also "addicted to speed." As a former math teacher, I know that students who rush through the process of solving math problems are usually the ones who get the wrong answers. It is hard to pay attention to details and be meticulous when working in a hurry. When I was a math teacher, before and during a test, I used to say to my students,

"Do not rush guys. This is not a competition. You still have a lot of time. Even if you finished the test, please go back and check your answers. You need to work meticulously!"

Dr. Lourdes Ferrer

REASON # 10

Acquiring new math knowledge is like constructing a multi-level building.

It is our belief that one of the greatest reasons why students dislike math and perform so poorly in standardized tests is because their math foundation is weak and they have numerous knowledge gaps. Most of us agree that acquiring new math knowledge, in many ways, is like constructing a multi-level building. The stability and strength of each floor depends on the one underneath. One of *Bleck & Bleck Architects* blogs states, "When a foundation is plumb and level, everything that goes on top of it will be simpler to install."

In one of my ACT Math Prep courses that I facilitated few weeks ago, a student who appeared to be anxious and frustrated with himself said to me,

> *"I know that I should know everything you are going over because I have seen it before. I just do not remember how to do it. I cannot believe I am taking Trigonometry this year and still feel that I am not prepared for this test."*

When you are reading an article, browsing and scanning can give you a good idea of what the article is all about; however, math is different. Instead of drifting through their math courses, students must master every concept and skill they learn. Like a building, the higher the level of the math course students take, the stronger their math foundation will have to be. Ms. Holly, one of the teachers that Arturo Ballines [co-writer] interviewed believes that,

> *"Students find math difficult because there are building blocks in math. You must learn a lesson and be able to properly use the information learned in order to move to the next lesson, which is the reason why students fall behind."*

Melany Carrillo [Co-writer] believes that this lack of ability to remember affects students' performance in other classes that could require a good math foundation. Physics, for example, is a science class that many students take during their senior year. To do well in this class, students must master basic Algebra 1 concepts and algorithms. Regarding this, a physics teacher that Melanie interviewed said,

> *"No matter what level you teach at, it's always the level before you, the one who screwed up. It can be that, what is holding students back in a physics class, is not knowing how to rearrange an equation to solve for the variable. You should had learned that stuff when you took Algebra 1, which a lot of you people, took during your first year in high school. Now I have you as a junior and still struggling with simple equations."*

It is this physics teacher's belief that the problem with math low performance is that students are passing their math classes because teachers cannot fail them. The following year they start already behind, which makes things more difficult for both the student and the new teacher. It is his belief that, "Math is easy to fall behind but hard to catch up!"

I always recommend my students to continue taking higher levels of math courses. However, only students with a strong math foundation can do this. Like erecting a tall building, students will not do well in their next math level class if they did not master the content of the previous course.

Dr. Lourdes Ferrer

REASON # 11

Teachers might not have the math competency needed to teach math with confidence and passion, especially at the K-5 grade levels.

One of the greatest challenges that educational leaders and school reformers are facing today is raising the content-expertise of teachers. According to authorities in the field of education, content-expertise is crucial to deliver quality instruction. Unfortunately, most of the professional development opportunities available to teachers focus on other classroom-related issues such as a culturally relevant instruction, classroom management, or the implementation of a new curricular program. Most math teachers, for example, do not have the opportunity to study, review or sharpen their algebra, geometry or statistics skills, which can lower their ability to demonstrate high levels of math competency while teaching. Regarding this, Arturo Ballines [co-writer] said,

> *"Teachers can make a lesson appear more complicated than it needs to be, which results in class confusion. Even though it is not the teachers' intentions to confuse*

students, unfortunately, they do so because they do not quite comprehend the lesson themselves."

While providing consulting services to numerous high schools across the nation, I have learned that most math teachers do not have the opportunity to study the standardized tests that their students will take for either school accountability or college admission purposes. For example, most high school math teachers have not seen or experienced taking an ACT or SAT math practice test, at least for a long time. If they had the opportunity to do so, I assure you that they would modify their instruction in such a way that could better prepare students to pass these high-stake tests.

This need for content-expertize is usually more evident at the elementary school level. Many elementary school teachers do not have the math knowledge and skills to teach the rigorous math content that students are now required to learn. Most teachers would rather deal with their lack of math content-expertise on their own in fear of being perceived by their administrators as unqualified teachers. Not long ago, a veteran Kindergarten teacher said to me,

> *"I have to teach math concepts that I never had to in my twenty-plus years of experience as a Kindergarten teacher. My students are working on algebraic and statistics concepts. They are finding the unknown in an equation and using data to build graphs. What happened to counting up to 100?"*

REASON # 12

Students do not have the grit needed to overcome challenges.

In my 30-plus years of experience as an educator, I have learned that one of the greatest reasons for students' negative attitude towards mathematics and low performance in the math section of most (if not all) standardized tests is their lack of grit. In psychology, grit is character trait that provides individuals the passion they need to pursue long-term goals and the motivation to achieve their respective objectives.

According to Angela L. Duckworth, IQ (Intellectual Quotient) is not the only factor (or variable) that separates students who achieve academic success from those who struggle academically. Gritty students have the drive and the stamina to work through challenges, failures, and adversity to achieve their academic goals, especially in hard-core subjects such as mathematics. She believes that students' level of grit is the greatest predictor of their level of math proficiency.

Let us be real! Math is not an easy academic subject. For many students, math is their most challenging class and to overcome its challenges, they will definitely need grit. This is especially true, or more evident, when they go beyond Arithmetic and start learning content and solving math problems that involve variables or "unknown" values. Most students are reporting that math became "a problem" when they enrolled in an Algebra class or were exposed, for the first time, to algebraic concepts. A very concerned mom once said to me,

> *"I do not know what happen! My son used to like math until he went to middle school and took an Algebra class. He was very good in adding, subtracting, multiplying or dividing numbers, fractions and even decimals. When the letters (variables) came in, there is when things got bad. I could not help him anymore. This thing about finding the value of x is not easy."*

Math also can be very challenging because it involves higher cognitive levels. According to the revised Boom's taxonomy, the five cognitive levels are remembering, understanding, applying, analyzing and creating. In many academic subjects, students must remember and understand what they learned; but in mathematics, students must apply what they learned and through analysis come up with the right answer to a problem. In other words, they must create an answer, which by nature is a challenge.

We could ask ourselves, "What fuels or creates grit?" Students who have the determination to achieve a goal are the ones who believe that what they pursue is worth pursuing. In other words, they value what they pursue so much that they are willing to do whatever it takes to achieve it. They are willing to sacrifice!

Students also develop grit when they have a "growth" mindset, not a "fixed" mindset. While students with a fixed mindset believe that their genes already predetermined whatever they will achieve, students with a growth mindset believe that the effort they put into learning (or their hard work) will determine their level of academic success.

Crystal Magana [co-writer] believes that the right mindset can help students overcome the fear of failure that they have regarding mathematics. In her own word,

> "I had a bad attitude towards math. It was like confronting my worst enemy. I was not aware that a positive attitude, diligence and hard work could lead to academic success. Although I wish I learned this before, I realized that I could still change my attitude. I knew that spending more time learning math was hard work. I still fear giving the wrong answer, and so do many people, even the top students. Nevertheless, there are ways we can all overcome this fear."

Melany Carrillo [co-author], passionately states that the level of math proficiency that students can reach will mostly depend on themselves. When you have grit, you are willing to do whatever it takes. She implied this when she said,

"The students' levity towards math can mostly be blamed on themselves. I believe that if you want to succeed, you will succeed. Like any other goal, academic success will require determination and arduous effort to defeat obstacles and overcome challenges. At the end, this is all about you."

Fernanda Valencia [co-writer], strongly feels that to excel in math students must make it a priority. Nothing should deter them from reaching their goals. In her own word,

"When we put our priorities in order and establish that our education is more important than whatever others may think of us, then we can become better learners. I know that mathematics is a hard, challenging and tedious subject, but as Dr. Lourdes always says, "We need to suck it up and deal with it!"

In conclusion, mathematics is an academic subject that demands hard work and hard work will require grit "fuel." We can say that grit is the "chemical reaction" between valuing an academic goal, having the right mindset to achieve it and making it a priority.

STRATEGIES TO OVERCOME APATHY AND IMPROVE PERFORMANCE

Dr. Lourdes Ferrer

STRATEGY # 1

Prior to implementation, find out the staff's perceptions regarding any new initiate to improve students' performance in mathematics.

I strongly believe that before introducing any kind of new initiative to improve students' performance in math, the district/school administration should investigate the staff's perceptions regarding the changes they are considering implement.

Let us be real! There will always be staff members who resist change. Through questionnaires, informal interviews, focus groups,

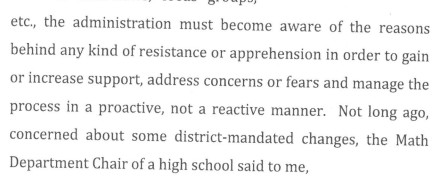

etc., the administration must become aware of the reasons behind any kind of resistance or apprehension in order to gain or increase support, address concerns or fears and manage the process in a proactive, not a reactive manner. Not long ago, concerned about some district-mandated changes, the Math Department Chair of a high school said to me,

"What I hate the most about teaching is that there is always something new forced down our throats! The administration is this district does not care about how we feel about anything. Don't you think we deserve to know what is going to happen before it happens? They would get more buy in and support from teachers if they would simply take our opinions in consideration."

STRATEGY # 2

Facilitate focus groups or meetings to create awareness regarding students' lack of math proficiency and develop solutions to address their math academic needs.

The school administration could facilitate focus group conversations with students, parents and teachers to:

a. Discuss the possible reasons behind students' apathy towards mathematics.

b. Analyze students' performance on the math portion of the standardized tests they took.

c. Develop solutions to improve students' attitudes and performance.

The purpose of these focus group conversations (or meetings) is to create awareness about the importance of students reaching math proficiency and come up with some  school wide strategies to improve students' attitude towards this subject and their performance on the standardized tests they must take. As a tricycle needs three wheels, the American Education System needs the collaboration of students, teachers and parents to function properly.

I am in owe of the number of teachers, parents and high school students who are completely clueless about our nation's widespread apathy towards math and low performance in the states' accountability and college entrance tests. Few weeks ago, I asked one of the mothers who attended one of my *In the Driver's Seat* seminars, "Out of everything you learned this evening, what got your attention the most?" Her response was,

> *"I have never seen those graphs before! I did not know that Hispanic students were doing so badly in the state's test. I have three kids in this district and they take that test every year. However, I never knew how well they did. Those reports they send home are too hard to understand. If I knew then what I learned today, my attitude towards that test would have been different. I am concerned!"*

STRATEGY # 3

Provide teachers with staff development opportunities in which they can increase their math level of proficiency.

District and school administrations could provide staff development opportunities in which teachers, especially at the elementary school level, can develop or increase their level of math proficiency. The purpose of these trainings is to  empower teachers to teach mathematics with greater content expertize and confidence. The content of these workshops must include the five NCTM (National Council of Teachers of Mathematics) standards, which are *Number and Operations, Algebra, Geometry, Measurement and Data Analysis and Probability,* with a focus on how these content areas are assessed on the state's accountability test. It is imperative that these math workshops are delivered:

a. In a rush-free manner to ensure that, teachers have ample time to practice with their colleagues what they learned.

b. In a stress-free manner, so teachers do not have to deal with thoughts and emotions that could affect their learning or classroom climate.

c. By content-experts and experienced k-12 teachers who have the ability to inspire, motivate and engage teachers in the learning process.

We must understand that it is not easy for teachers to admit that they need help. They, like many students, might fear being perceived by their administrators (or colleagues) as unqualified to teach or unable to help students improve their performance in math. Not long ago, during one of my CCC-PARCC (Common Core Standards and Partnership for Assessment of Readiness for College and Career) trainings, concerned about the district's new math curriculum, one of the k-5 teachers expressed,

> "I have done a great job helping students improve their reading skills. I love to read! However, teaching mathematics is a different story. The math we must teach now is so much harder than years ago. I have a hard time solving most of the sample PARCC items. Math has never been my forte. I promise you that I am not the only teacher who feels this way."

Even high school teachers, who are certified in mathematics, are expressing the need to sharpen their math skills, especially when they are assigned to teach a math course different from the one they are accustomed to teach. Reflecting on what she learned during one of my workshops, an experienced high school math teacher said to me,

"I have been teaching Algebra 1 for the past five years. I just learned that I would teach Geometry next year, which is a very different course. I will definitely need some kind of training to prepare myself to teach this or any other math class that I could be assigned to teach next year. I just wished the district would give us the opportunity to sharper our skills, especially during summer time."

Dr. Lourdes Ferrer

STRATEGY # 4

Require staff members to go through standardized test-simulations.

We strongly recommend that, early in the school year, the district administration provides all instructional staff members (including themselves) the opportunity to participate in test-simulations. These simulations must be similar in length, administration  process, content, format and rigor to the tests students will have to take. The idea is for teachers to experience what students go through when they are tested so they are better prepared to help students improve.

The three pillars of any teaching-learning process are standards, instruction and assessment. These three must be aligned in order for the process to work effectively. Among many other things, educators who go through these test-simulations are able to see the type of item, rigor level and the pressure of time that students are under when they take the test. This insight could empower educators to instruct and asses their students in a way that is aligned to the standardized tests that students take. That way, teachers do not have to stop teaching their curriculum to prepare students for these tests – allowing them to move away from "teaching to the test" to "testing what they teach."

Few months ago, I asked an 8th grade student who came with his mom to one of my parent workshops, "How well did you do on the ISAT (Illinois Standards Assessment test)?" His response was:

> *"That test is so hard! The whole school stopped everything just to prepare us for that test. We worked so hard for nothing. The questions are different from the questions we get in class. First, the clock is ticking; so I do not have as much time as I have in class. Second, the questions are so much harder. It feels like they are testing us on things we never covered in class."*

STRATEGY # 5

Increase student assessment literacy and help them develop up-to-date test-taking skills.

We highly recommend that schools design and facilitate classroom lessons in which students can learn the purpose, administration process, format and the use of standardized tests. Most students go through the process of testing not  knowing why they are doing so. Test preparation, in my opinion, needs to be an on-going classroom activity. It should be integrated into all academic subjects because assessment is a key component of our educational system.

The main purpose of a classroom lesson like this is to increase student assessment literacy so they can be better prepared to achieve academic success. This kind of training must be delivered as early as possible during the school year, not just before any high stake standardized test.

Not all staff members are qualified to do this. Content-expertize does not necessarily translate into test-taking expertize. At the minimum, staff members who provide this kind of training must have a positive attitude towards the test they are preparing students to take.

During a high school focus group that I facilitated some years ago, the students shared with me that the teachers that were preparing them for the state's accountability were complaining about it. They did not believe in the test because they consider it an unfair measure of the teachers' quality of instruction. It is very hard for students to prepare for a test that teachers do not believe in.

It is imperative that teachers who facilitate these trainings also have the knowledge, skills and ability to explain every item in the practice test. This is not easy! It requires content-mastery and great communication skills. By experience, I know that during my ACT math prep courses, not only I have to understand the math problems but also know how to solve them in many different ways. Every student is different and "one size does not fit all."

Instructors who provide test preparation must be aware of the emotional and social factors that can affect students' learning. Some students, for example, do not believe in their ability to learn, lack the motivation they need to work hard or are overwhelmed with test fear or anxiety. I good test prep instructor can help students develop the mental frame of reference they need to overcome thoughts and feeling that could affect their performance in any testing situation.

Test prep teachers must also go beyond telling or explaining students what to do. Students need ample time to practice during the training the test taking strategies they are learning. We must be aware that the strategies that worked in the past might not be as effective anymore. Instead of multiple-choice items, many assessment companies are designing performance items. These items require that students demonstrate their work and/or write the answer instead of choosing from series of alternatives. For example, the popular "make an educated guess" strategy does not work with performance items.

We are moving away from paper and pencil to computerized tests. These types of tests require computer-related skills. The feeling of turning a page and bubbling in an answer on a Scantron card is very different from scrolling down and clicking or typing an answer. Taking this in consideration, if the test is a computer-based assessment, then the preparation must include opportunities in which students can learn and practice the computer skills they need to demonstrate their knowledge.

Testing is a big component of our educational system. More than ever before, mastering the content and skills tested in any assessment is as important as being good test-takers.

STRATEGY # 6

Increase students' awareness regarding high-in-demand college degrees that require a strong foundation in mathematics.

We believe that a significant reason for students' apathy towards mathematics and low performance on high stake standardized test is that they do not see the usefulness or the advantages of reaching math proficiency. Many of them do not know that most (if not all) of the high in demand degrees, require a strong foundation in mathematics.  This is why we believe that school districts must facilitate, or enroll their students to participate in events in which students, especially at the middle and high school levels, can learn and be exposed to careers that are in great demand.

The purpose of events like these is to help students understand the positive correlation that exists between math proficiency and earning degrees that lead to new and interesting high-paying careers.

Students must also become aware that a significant number of high school graduates who enroll in college are required to take math prep courses. Due to their poor performance on college entrance tests such as the ACT or SAT, they end up wasting time, energy and money in courses that do not count towards a college degree. Disappointed by this, many of them dropout when they find themselves learning in college what they should had learned in high school.

The lack of math proficiency also deter students from enrolling in college academic programs that include high-level of math courses. During all my *Grooming for Excellence* seminars, I always ask students to share the degrees that they are planning to pursue. It is concerning how little they know about all the degrees that lead to high in demand careers. At least, 50% of them are either planning to major in psychology, sociology or elementary school education. In their own words, "I like to work with people (or children) and I want to make a difference in other people's lives." Little do they know that, although their intentions are noble and these degrees are wonderful, they are likely to end up in low-paying jobs that do not require a college education, or has nothing to do with what they studied. Regarding this, Christian Ramirez [co-writer] wrote,

> *"A question that many students tend to ask is, 'Why is math so important in life?' The answer to the question may vary; however, the answer that I want to give is that*

if you want to earn a lot of money in your job, you will need to study a competitive degree. Do you know what? Competitive degrees are likely to require students to take high-level math courses in college. That means that you need math if you want to earn a lot of money. Some examples of jobs that require a lot of math and pay the most are engineering and anything in the sciences, including health sciences."

Dr. Lourdes Ferrer

STRATEGY # 7

Create a school culture that embraces a growth-mindset versus a fixed-mindset.

One of the greatest truths that I have learned in my 30-plus years of experience working with students is that their mindset regarding learning will determine what and how much they learn. This is why the 18 students who

participated in this book, Deborah and I highly strongly recommend that the district and/or school administration put in place a plan to help students, parents and even teachers embrace a growth-mindset versus a fixed-mindset.

Students with a fixed mindset attribute academic achievement to factors beyond their control. They think that, if they have to work hard to learn, then they do not have the ability to excel in school. On the other hand, students with growth mindset believe that intelligence, or the ability to learn, is something that can be cultivated. Students with a growth mindset are certain that the more they challenge themselves the smarter they can become.

Since three of the greatest components of any culture are the values, beliefs and perceptions, to create a school culture that embraces a growth-mindset, students, teachers and parents must learn to:

- ✓ Value hard work or a strong work ethic more than their "genes" or innate traits;
- ✓ Believe in their ability to learn, not that some people can learn and others cannot; and,
- ✓ Perceive challenges or setbacks as opportunities to learn and grow, not as reasons to avoid and escape.

Changing people' values, believes and perceptions will require time and indoctrination, or good "brainwashing" at all levels. Although it is possible, like any other initiative, it will require planning, strategizing, monitoring, etc.

I have learned that instilling or changing students' believes and perceptions regarding anything is best done when they are young. For example, when I am visiting my grandchildren, I cannot mix non-recyclable with recyclable garbage. In my grandson's words, "Abuela [grandmother], don't you want to save the planet?" If I grab a chocolate chip cookie, I will be reminded of its high sugar content. Trust me! They learned that in school, not at home.

In conclusion, the same way that children learn in school that they must recycle to protect the planet and eat right and exercise to live healthy lives, they can also learn that "smart" is not just something that they are, but something they can become through effective effort.

Dr. Lourdes Ferrer

STRATEGY # 8

Normalize asking questions during classroom instruction.

The fear of asking questions during classroom instruction was identified by the students as one of the leading reasons for low performance in mathematics. Students do not see or view asking questions as a normal and key  component of the teaching-learning process. That is why we highly recommend that schools come up with a strategic plan to normalize asking questions, eliminate fears and increase classroom participation.

On one hand, we have students who are reluctant to ask questions because they fear being perceived by their peers as unintelligent or "not smart enough" to take the class. On the other hand, we have others that think that asking questions could show "too much" interest in learning and then be viewed by their peers as nerds or geeks. We even learned through the interviews that there are students who fear annoying their teachers by "interrupting" the class flow with their questions. In their minds, asking question can impede teachers' ability to complete the lesson or cover the material they should for that day.

Students must learn to value the practice of asking questions. They need to see it as a normal and healthy classroom activity that could benefit all students in class. When I was a high school math teacher, I counteracted the fear of asking questions by correcting attitudes and behaviors that deterred students from participating in class and celebrating or recognizing those students who overcame their fear of being criticized or rejected by their peers.

Teachers, in my opinion, are more powerful than they think they are! Pre-K to 5th grade teachers have been successful in instilling in young minds values, beliefs and perceptions that lead to positive behavioral changes regarding many aspects of their lives. For example, teachers have reoriented our children's views regarding what to eat. Today's children believe that, "Eating vegetables and fruits can keep you healthy" more than, "Eating meat and potatoes can make you stronger," like in the old days.

I am convinced that we educators have the ability to help students see asking questions as a normal and healthy classroom activity instead of a of a class disruption or an activity that could lead to embarrassment.

Dr. Lourdes Ferrer

STRATEGY # 9

Provide after school opportunities in which students can improve their math proficiency and/or prepare for the math portion of high-stake standardized tests.

The students who participated in this study consistently expressed the need to provide students with after school opportunities in which they can develop better math skills or prepare for high  stake tests such as the SAT and ACT. It is their opinion that no matter how motivated they are to learn math and do well on these tests, the amount of time students spend in class is not enough to master the content or prepare for college entrance tests. Although they wished their teachers could teach at a slower pace, they understand that teachers are pressured to cover (and complete) their course curriculums. This is why we believe that all students could benefit if their schools could provide after-school or weekend opportunities to:

a. Offer students who will participate in high stake assessments or college admission exams test-prep courses.

> It is the students' belief that the items (or questions) in college admission exams are different from the problems they are used to solving in their math classes. According to a high school student who just took the ACT test,
>
>> *"Although I am taking a pre-calculus class and I usually Ace every test, I saw problems in that test that I have never seen before."*

b. Provide students who are struggling in class the opportunity to take the same class all over again, hopefully with the same teacher.

> Students think that taking the same class again or listening to the same content all over again, could help them catch key concepts that they could have missed. In Deborah Ferrer's words,
>
>> *"It is like watching a movie for the second time. You will be surprised how much you missed the first time you saw it."*

c. Give students who missed instructional time or are going through especial circumstances the opportunity to be tutored by skilled and caring peers or teachers so they can catch up with the rest of the class.

> It is students' belief that there are learning gaps and circumstances that are unique to each individual student and cannot be addressed in class. Regarding this, a high school student who missed class because of illness said,

"I was able to pass my Geometry class because of the tutoring I was receiving after I came back to school. Sometimes, especially in difficult times, you need someone to be there just for you."

Dr. Lourdes Ferrer

STRATEGY # 10

Recognize and celebrate students who excel or improve in mathematics.

In order to improve students' attitudes towards mathematics and their performance in any standardized test, I believe we should recognize and celebrate students who excel or improve their performance in mathematics. Many students complain that students, who excel in sports, or in any of the performance arts, are much more recognized or celebrated than those who excel in the academics, especially at the high school level.

During a student focus group that I facilitated years ago in a low performance high school in Florida, I asked the students what they believed their school could do to improve student performance on the *FCAT (Florida Comprehensive Assessment Test)*; and, to share their thoughts in writing. It took me by surprise the high level of frustration they expressed in their written responses. They all agreed that their school consistently paid too much attention to their football, basketball or wrestling teams. Those who exceled in the academics received little to no recognition from the administration. One student in particular wrote:

> *"In the morning announcements all you hear is about how well the team played the night before. The whole school is there when there is a game screaming at the top of their lungs. Not only are the parents there but also the administration. You never hear about how well a student did on the ACT or a student who won a speech state competition. If you are a real good student, you can join the Honor Society and hopefully be invited to a breakfast where you get a Certificate of Achievement. That is all you will get."*

Celebrating academic success, especially in mathematics, is key to get more students to embrace this

science. Among many other things, students who are recognized or celebrated see the fruit or outcome of their hard work; reflect on the steps they took to achieve; and, are motivated to repeat the behaviors that let to their success.

Students are more likely to remain engaged and produce high quality academic work. Because it is only human to seek some kind of recognition, these kinds of activities can motivate other students to improve their behavior and academic performance in order to get the same acknowledgement that their peers are receiving.

Dr. Lourdes Ferrer

STRATEGY # 11

Display throughout the building and in classrooms visuals and objects that could motivate students to pursue higher levels of math proficiency.

During my long career in education, I have learned that a short walk through the halls of any school can give me a good idea regarding what the staff and school administration values. Improving students' attitude towards mathematics and their performance on standardized tests will require that we introduce into the school culture the values, beliefs and perceptions regarding mathematics that lead to improved  performance. There is a Chinese proverb that says, "One picture is worth ten thousand words," which means that complex ideas can be conveyed with just a single image. I believe that a good way to change students' attitude towards anything is through visual exhibitions. It is for this reason that I recommend that schools display throughout the building (and in classrooms) objects or visuals that clearly convey or send a positive massage regarding mathematics.

The displays in most buildings, especially at the high school level, are pictures of students playing an instrument, participating in sports or acting in a school play. When I visit their media centers, I see posters of celebrities who enjoy reading, which is a great way to show that even Hollywood celebrities value reading. I might see the pictures of students who are part of the Honor Society or the valedictorian of previous graduating classes. What I hardly see are visuals that:

a. Promote the relevance and importance of reaching math proficiency;

b. Create awareness that high-in-demand degrees require a strong foundation in math; and,

c. Recognize students who excel or have significantly improved in mathematics.

Few weeks ago, during one of my *Grooming for Excellence* seminars, a high school student publicly said,

> *"If math is so important, why is it that we never see any kind of recognition, like pictures of students that did awesome on the ACT? My friend scored like a 30 in the math portion of this test, which is a lot higher than the passing score and yet, there is nothing about him for everyone to see. You just see big pictures of kids scoring a touchdown or shooting a 3-point in a basketball game. Don't you think a 30 on the ACT deserves more credit than a touchdown? If you want to be recognized, I guess math is not the right path."*

STRATEGY # 12

Provide parents with family-friendly strategies that they can use to help their children improve their math performance.

Researchers in the field of school reform seem to agree that parent involvement is one of the leading indicator of student academic success. When parents are involved, their children reach higher levels of academic proficiency. Therefore, if we want to improve students' attitude  towards mathematics and their performance in any testing situation, we need to empower parents to support their children's math education.

Let us accept the fact that parents from some ethnic groups support their children's education more than parents from others do; and some home environments are more conducive to academic success than others are. Intrigued about this reality, Amairin Dominguez [co-writer] asked Ms Love (one of her teachers), "Why do you think Asian and White students are likely to outperform Hispanics and Asians?" Although her teacher's response was not what Amairin expected to hear, she agreed with her. According to Ms. Love:

> *"As a teacher, it feels good to get credit for students' high performance; however, it also hurts to take the blame when they fail. Nevertheless, the parents, not the teachers, are the leading contributors of their own children's academic success or failure. Good parenting will result in student success no matter what schools or teachers do. Race has absolutely nothing to do with a child's success."*

To increase parent involvement, I recommend that school administrators (and teachers) plan, design and implement family-friendly strategies to provide parents with the awareness, knowledge and skills they need to help their children improve their math proficiency.

First, parents need to become more aware of the importance of mathematics in their children academic development and post-secondary education. We cannot assume that all parents know that math proficiency, among many other things, helps students develop the problem solving skills and the level of confidence they need to excel in school. Parents must also know that most of the high-in-demand degrees also require a strong foundation in mathematics. Because all parents want their children to be successful in life, they are likely to do whatever it takes to ensure that they do so.

Second, the school staff needs to help parents embrace a growth-mindset versus a fixed mindset. Parents with a fixed-mindset do not encourage their children to put effort because in their minds, their children are stuck with whatever intelligence they were born with. For them, their children's failure in math means that they do not have the intelligence to pass the class successfully. On the other hand, parents with a growth-mindset will encourage their children to commit and work hard because overcoming challenges will make them smarter. They believe that "smart" or intelligent is something that their children can become through continuous effective effort.

Third, parents need to learn how to create a home environment that is favorable for learning. We cannot assume that parents know how that environment looks like or how to create it. Some family-friendly strategies that parents can implement to support their children's math education are:

a. Facilitate a place at home for their children to study and complete their homework assignments

b. Provide their children a consistent study time free of distractions

c. Supervise daily homework to warrant that is completed with integrity

d. Connect with their children's math teachers in a positive and productive manner so they can reach out for help if needed

Through well-designed family workshops, schools can empower and train parents to provide their children the kind of support they need to excel in math. Only properly-trained staff members, who have the ability to effectively communicate with parents, should deliver this type of training. Since educating parents is very different from educating children, it is important that these parent workshops are facilitated using Adult Education Best Practices.

Parents can also learn how to help their children improve their math performance through school-recommended books, videos and brochures. Through phone, text and emails blasts, schools can also communicate to parent ideas or strategies in capsulized manner. The idea is to use different ways of communication to continuously empower parents throughout the year. The same way that no one learns how to play the guitar in a single lesson, it will take more than one event or strategy to empower parents to do what they need to do at home to ensure that their children reach math proficiency.

FINAL THOUGHTS

I truly hope that after reading *Math Phobia: Strategies to Overcome Apathy and Improve Performance,* you have gained a greater level of insight regarding our nation's widespread apathy towards mathematics and students' low performance in the math portion of state, national and international standardized tests. I would like you to spend a few minutes reflecting on the following three questions:

a. How do you feel about our students' math phobia and low performance?

b. How important do you think it is to change this apathy and low performance trend?

c. What role do you play, or would like to play, in helping more students embrace math and demonstrate their proficiency through standardized tests?

I know that changing students' values, beliefs and perceptions regarding math is not an easy task. Improving their performance will require time, effort and collaboration. The same way that a tricycle needs three wheels to run properly, the American Education System needs the collaboration of students, teachers and parents in order to fulfill its purpose - ensure our children's employability and strengthen our nation's ability to compete in a global economy. I really believe that working together we can help students overcome the challenges that prevent them from experiencing success in math. It can be done!

First, let's boldly create awareness among students, teachers, and parents regarding the important role that math plays in students' academic development. They must understand the correlation that exists between math proficiency and career success in our Digital Era.

Second, let's implement the recommendations presented in this book or create teams of academic experts to brainstorm and come up with new ways to help students improve. We understand that "one size does not fit all." One strategy or recommendation might not be appropriate for all schools.

As a nation, we must do whatever it takes to increase the percent of students who excel in mathematics; eliminate the stubborn performance gaps that exist between ethnic groups; and, help our children move up the ladder in international assessments. For the sake of our children's future and our nation's standing in the world, join us in our effort to help more students see the relevance of math and reap its numerous benefits.

STUDENTS' ESSAYS

Dr. Lourdes Ferrer

Amairin Dominguez

I am a 16-year-old high school student writing this essay to state my opinions regarding students' apathy towards math and the reasons behind their poor performance on standardized tests. I have always had apathy towards math and never been very good at it; but I always try! My intention, through writing this essay, is to figure out why is it that I and many other students may have a problem with this subject. However, the real question is, "Why, according to the NAEP (National Assessment of Educational Progress) report, Asians and Whites have higher proficiency rates than Hispanics and African Americans, in all subjects tested, especially mathematics?"

What is math? Mathematics is the science that deals with the logic of shape, quantity and arrangement. According to LiveScience and LiveStrong, math is all around us and in everything, we do. It is the building block for everything in our daily lives, including mobile devices, architecture, art, money, engineering, and even sports. Math is critically involved in much of humanity's progress. It is impossible to conceive the progress we are making without mathematics. Unfortunately, that hardly makes students feel better if they do not believe that they are going to be contributing to that progress themselves. Why is math so important? Math teaches life skills, supports continuing careers, enhances education, and teaches logical and critical thinking.

Teacher Jacqui Rempala, from West Aurora High School, believes that the reason why students have an apathetic attitude towards math is that math does not provide instant gratification. In her own words, "Students have the privilege of looking up anything to get answers at the drop of a hat. Any topic that they want to know or read about, they Google it and thousands of sites pop up for them to click and begin finding answers." It is her belief that math is not always like this. Most math courses take time because students must solve problems, with multiple routes that could possibly lead to dead ends. She also stated, "I don't believe students really take much time to think of a game plan to reason through problems, and once they get stuck they just give up. Many students do not take the time to sit down and study for their tests; and, if it is not something that comes naturally or easy to them, they have a tendency to just give up."

I do believe another big reason for both apathy towards math and low test scores is that the curriculum that teachers must follow is too big. Teachers have many topics to teach but not enough time to teach; therefore, instead of really diving deep into a concept so that students can fully understand it, they graze the surface and move on. In her own words, "When I am teaching, I feel like I don't have a lot of time to really have the students interacting and discovering concepts that might interest them more because of what I am required to get through in a year."

A second reason for students' apathy towards math, according to the math teacher Kathi Straight is that, "Our mainstream society tells students that it is okay to not excel in math." This message is transmitted to us through the media, where it is ordinary to use math as a punch line. Parents tell their struggling math student that it is okay to not do well in math because they did not understand it either. I have even heard well-meaning elementary teachers tell kids, "It is okay not to understand math." Instead of working and supporting struggling students, teachers console them and accept their defeat. Think about this. No one says, "I cannot read." Actually, many adults hide the fact that they cannot read. They are embarrassed by their illiteracy. On the other hand, it is perfectly fine to tell the world, "I can't do math."

I was watching a home improvement show on television when a very intelligent homebuilder demonstrated a clear understanding of structural engineering and advanced carpentry through his work. I was shocked when he said, "I'm not good at science or math". If he truly were deficient in science and math, he would be unable to do his work. The homebuilder would not even give himself the credit! Teacher Straight said, "Students rise to the level of the expectations put in front of them. Students need to know that when they score well or show improvement, it gives them the power to open doors."

Ms. Straight believes that we need to stop comparing students with each other and instead we should focus on their individual growth. The reason why White and Asian students tend to outperform Hispanics and Blacks is the disparity in opportunities for these groups. If we look at a typical higher math class, you will see that it is predominantly white. Everyone expects more from students enrolled in higher math courses because these courses are more rigorous. Students are learning skills that students in standard math classes do not see. It is Straight's belief that, "The way we place students into accelerated classes is flawed. It focuses on what the student already knows rather than their potential for learning."

There are multitude reasons why American students develop such distaste to mathematics. The culture of the typical teen includes going out, sports, friends, and having fun. According to Straight, "There is a definite shift from school-centric attitudes to more of a blithely one in our thoughts on education as a whole. We did not cultivate our kids to be math-loving machines from a young age, resulting in the low performance we see today. Although I value children being able to explore their own thoughts, interests and hobbies, a bigger emphasis should be placed on the value and possibilities of actually wanting to go to school."

According to my mother Sue, "If we want all students to be more successful in math, the first thing that we must do is change the way math is taught." Students differ in the way they learn. There are sometimes big and small differences in learning styles between girls and boys. In her own words, "Addressing different ways of learning, additional explanations, visual examples, etc. would be very helpful and offer much more support to those who struggle. If a student feels successful, they will have a tendency to try harder and achieve more." It is her belief that these strategies apply to every ethnic group. If this were to occur, I think all groups would excel more. It may take additional teacher education, teacher replacement, and teachers with a passion for students to achieve success. The attitude needs to change on both sides of the teaching-learning process to see the kind of success we would all like to see, not only in math, but also in all subjects.

I believe Asian and White students usually outperform Hispanics and African Americans because of their home-culture. I think the majority of Asian and White parents strongly encourage good performance in their children's classes. They offer help and support at home, pay for tutors, etc. They also place importance on the value of getting a good education from the start. Unfortunately, many parents do not see the importance of receiving a good education.

According to Mr. Love, a teacher from West Aurora High School, schools need to emphasize improvement on the over-all self-esteem of the students. In her own words, "A hardworking student can overcome early deficits eventually if the school helps him realize that he can do well if he work for it. Working for an achievement and wanting to achieve are two different things. Working to improve can take years to catch up if a student is behind from the beginning. Because the beginning is so important, we need to have good preschools for everyone."

Parents need to be convinced that even when their children are in preschool, education is important! If they cannot or will not read to their kids, they must find someone who will. Students who lack reading ability in grade school are already behind; and if teachers teach to their level and do not push them to get better, then they end up not challenging the students who are ahead. It is important to challenge the students who are ahead, because the challenge is what makes it fun to learn.

David, an 18-year-old senior in High School, believes that major reforms are required to close achievement gaps, not only in math, but in all of the other critical academic areas as well. It is his own words, "We wonder why other countries such as Finland and Korea are skyrocketing ahead of us in education. It is not due to some magic water that they must be drinking. Racism against your own people derogates the slightest possibility of achievement through education. Education and knowledge are two of the most powerful possessions anyone can own, and historically, our country systematically has excluded minorities from gaining these possessions. By limiting their education, their resources and options are also limited. The oppressed group is lead to be ignorant of the fact that they are oppressed." In short, a wave of social equality movements would have to sweep the nation to inspire a generation to reach as high as they can. We are all humans. We all have an innate potential for growth when we are not limited by arbitrary restrictions.

There is always another side to a story. Teacher Matt Love, like many others, disagrees with the idea that students in general have apathy towards mathematics. Regarding this she said, "I think, especially on the ACT, most students care. Unfortunately, for some, they are taking a test that takes years of steady work to be ready to take. Realizing during their junior year that school is important does not give them enough time to do well." When I had asked Mr. Love why he believes that Asian and White students are likely to outperform Hispanics and African Americans, his answer was not what I expected, although I agree. He stated, "It is not a race issue at all. It is a home issue. If your family cares about school, they will read to you when you are young. The sooner you read the better you will do. As a teacher, it feels good to get credit for students' high performance; however, it also hurts to take the blame when they fail. Nevertheless, the parents, not the teachers, are the leading contributors of their own children's academic success or failure. How can we expect your child's school to be responsible for their upbringing? Good parenting will result in student success no matter what schools or teachers do. If my own two children were to do poorly in school, it would be my fault for not preparing them well. Race has absolutely nothing to do with a child's success." As you can see, it is my teacher's believe that home-culture is everything!

Studying this topic has opened my eyes to see that math may be more important than we think and that schools, teachers and students can all do more to improve students' attitude towards math as well as raise their scores in standardized tests. This really changes my perspective as a student who struggles with math. I learned to look for other perspectives, besides my own, in order to find other ways to help myself.

Arturo Ballines

I am a Hispanic student from West Aurora High School named Arturo Ballines. I am writing this paper to explore the reasons why many students dislike and are apathetic towards math. It is very concerning knowing that students dislike math because it does not come easy to them. It is not only affecting their confidence but their future goals as well. No student should hate math! Math is a very important subject to learn and students should understand the reason for it. After conducting a series of interviews and research online, I found out the three greatest reasons for high school students' apathy towards mathematics and low performance on standardized tests.

Before I state my reasons why students have apathy towards math, I need to inform you why math is so important. Math is essential to learning because all jobs require basic math skills. Math is the science that helps us understand logic, shape and arrangement. Math is required in several areas such as biology, technology, physics, chemistry and so much more. Without math, our world would not be how it is today. We humans are the most intelligent specie in the world and we were destined to understand the world that we live in. We would never have the different types of technology that we have today in our world if it was not for mathematics.

The first reason why many students create apathy towards math is the fact that many students do not understand the importance of learning the subject. Many students do not see how they would end up using such complex math in their future, causing them to react so negatively against the subject. Kathy, a former college student states, "Math teaches you some useful things; but I believe that math should pertain to something you will do in your future job." Unfortunately, many believe that math skills should only be learned if your career demands it, but isn't math a life skill also? What about if you want to change your career or become more employable? It is highly concerning that, students do not see the importance of math and its impact beyond how well they do on standardized tests. It can also limit career opportunities as well. Seeing students do poorly on standardized test scores is sad and heartbreaking because they begin to assume that they may not be successful in their future. In addition, students believe that it is acceptable to be bad at math, which is causing them to give inadequate effort towards learning the subject.

Ms. Robinson, who is a math teacher in high school, says that, "'Students are influenced by society." I have heard some parents say, "It is okay, I was never good at math either." It is not right for students to be thinking that it is okay. Students see how others are doing poorly in math assignments. Then they are influenced by their negative behaviors. Having students believe that it is okay to lack math skills is unacceptable.

Another important factor that contributes to why many students have apathy towards math is that students find math a challenging subject. Math has different lessons that compile on one another. Ms. Holly, who is an English teacher in high school said, "Students find math difficult because there are building blocks in math. You must learn a lesson and be able to properly use the information learned in order to move to the next lesson, which is the reason why students fall behind." Not understanding one lesson can lead a student to not understanding the next one, which is how math functions. After the teacher teaches a lesson, students still find it hard and give up on learning the information. When the same problems from the lesson appear on a standardized test, students begin to panic, sweat and scream in their heads. This tends to happen when students do not understand a lesson and decide to move on.

Math, at times, is difficult and stressful. The anxiety they are experiencing inhibits students from understanding the information they are learning, causing students to give up on learning it. Students observe other students who comprehend math better than they do and begin to feel unintelligent. When students start to lack confidence in themselves, they become unmotivated to keep trying. Instead of being motivated, they start being very negative against the subject and choose not to participate.

There are students that are stereotyped. They feel the pressure to meet what others expect from them. Everyone should put all of their effort towards learning the subject and not feel judged when they find some lessons challenging. Students also feel discouraged when they are placed in lower level classes. Mr. Raymond believes that, "Students who get placed in lower level classes feel 'dumb' and think that they will be unsuccessful, which is not true. Students should keep trying, not giving up, and doing their best." I believe that, as long as students are consistent towards their work and effort, they will do well and be successful.

The third reason why students have apathy towards math is that they do not always have a good teacher. Young students need a fun and motivating teacher, which is a problem. Not all teachers are fun and motivating. Ms. Finley, who is a high school math teacher said, "Teachers need to be encouraging. They need to keep everyone interested, engaged in the lesson, and have everyone's eyes up and paying attention. They also need to be better teachers. Teachers need to find easier and better ways to teach." Math teachers who teach a class insipidly tend to have fewer students interested in the lesson. Amy, a student in my high school simply says, "There are some teachers that just cannot teach well and others that are too boring. There are some teachers that know what they are doing and they know how to teach the lesson with less confusion; however, there are others that just make it look too complex." Teachers can make a lesson appear more complicated than it needs to be, which results in class confusion. Even though it is not the teachers' intentions to confuse students, unfortunately, they do so because they do not quite comprehend the lesson themselves. Sometimes, the way teachers see what they are teaching is different from the way students see it. Students do not like walking into the same math class every day, with the same teacher, who appears to be talking to himself throughout the whole period. It is important for teachers to be familiar with the different ways students learn in order to keep them interested.

There are also students who are not assertive enough to ask questions to the teachers. They feel uncomfortable with the teacher or they feel like the teacher will be disappointed for not being able to understand such a simple problem. Sometimes when students ask the teacher for a little more help, they still end up not understanding the problem. They are afraid to ask the teacher again because some teachers are impatient. This is true! I believe that students should not be afraid to ask questions. It is the teachers' fault because they are not teaching clearly enough and do not show that they care about each individual student.

One way the schools can improve the students' attitude towards math is by informing students how it will affect them in their future careers. It is important for teachers to apply math to real life. Teachers should teach students why they need to learn such formulas and other equations. When students understand why they are required to learn math, they begin to take more interest in the subject resulting in more effort and higher test scores. Dr. Hall states that, "Students do not connect math to real life. They need to understand why it is necessary to know math." Students need to see how math affects our society each day and teachers should be the ones in charge of informing their students why they are learning what they are learning.

Another way that schools can improve students' attitude towards math is by allowing foreign students to take standardized tests in their preferred language. There are foreign students in our country that give all their effort but they still have trouble understanding English. The language barrier is affecting their tests scores, not their lack of math skills. Ms. Holly says, "I have Hispanic students who are more comfortable speaking Spanish because it is the first language that they learned. It is their preferred language. Hispanic students should be given the option to take any standardized test in Spanish." Students who are better at a language other than English should have the option to choose the language that they would rather take the test in. Giving students a language option when they take standardized tests will help the scores go up. Students will feel more confident, not only in math, but in other subjects as well.

Finally yet importantly, schools should hire better teachers who actually care about teaching their students. Schools need better teachers who love to teach and love to show their passion for teaching. Teachers should be more enthusiastic and have their students' attention throughout the whole class. Teachers need to keep everyone's attention, even if it means jumping off walls, running around the classroom or even breaking a leg, as long as they keep the students focused and paying attention. Kathy also says, "Schools need motivating teachers that show that they care. They need better teaching methods and give individual help." Teachers need to set better examples and teach math with better methods by having students be more engaged in the lesson. Amy says, "As a student, I learn better when I am doing activities such as using the white board or playing fun math games that are related to the lesson." Teachers need to include fun activities in the class in order for everyone to be engaged in the lesson and better understand it. Teachers should also give students individual help. Teachers should be aware of the students who find a lesson challenging and ask where they are having the most trouble in. Teachers are the ones who are going to change students' lives and it is their responsibility that their students are all learning the material by teaching students the best way possible.

In conclusion, I hope I kept your interest throughout this whole paper I provided you with information regarding students' apathy towards math and what schools can do to improve their attitude. Students generate hatred against math when they do not find a reason to be learning the material. It is the teachers' job to apply math to real life situations. Teachers need to show the use of every equation and formula students learn. Students also have apathy towards math when they find it challenging and hard. Teachers need to improve the class environment so students can have a more positive attitude towards math and do better. Furthermore, students begin to have apathy towards math when their teacher make the lesson appear more complex than it needs to be. Teachers need to better improve their teaching skills and be more enthusiastic in order for students to understand the material and do great. These are my three reasons why students create apathy towards math and what schools can do to improve their attitude. Thank you for reading this paper.

Ashley McCoy

Why do we Americans complain about hating math so much? It is not just students disliking math; it is the entire American population. It starts when you are younger in elementary school learning how to add, subtract, multiply and divide. Then when you grow older, you move on to middle and high school. Once you get into high school, the teachers teach you things like algebra II and trigonometry, which you think you do not need to learn and it is just a waste of time. Well, I thought the same thing until I realized that math is everywhere. Everything that you do involves math. If you like shopping, like me, and want to buy the whole store, then you're going to have to know how much everything is going to be, how much tax you are going to be charged, and what interest you're going to be paying if you are using a credit card. After conducting a series of interviews and researching online, I found that there are three major reasons for high school students' apathy towards mathematics and low performance on standardized tests. Students lack time to put the necessary effort; see mathematics as a subject irrelevant to their lives and future career plans; and, the math is a subject difficult to engage in a fun and creative way.

The first reason for high school students' apathy towards mathematics and low performance on standardized tests is students' lack of time to put in the necessary effort. There is too much to do! A student from West Aurora High School said, "They freak out during a test because it's a test given to determine how much knowledge they are supposed to know." Students feel overwhelmed when teachers give them a specific time to do something; so they feel like they should not put all the effort into something they know they are not going to be able to finish. It is not right for the teachers to time students when each student develops and learns at their own individual pace. Most students do not put effort into their work because the teacher assigns too much for them to do, all in one night.

Another teacher from West Aurora High School said, "The students today are dealing with too many problems outside of school like poverty, broken relationships, and family problems that when it comes to taking a standardized test, it's a big worry." It is this teacher's belief that students have so much going on in their life that many people do not know of. Some students only have one parent, and some do not even have parents. They might live with an aunt, an uncle or a grandparent. "I know someone that lost a parent at a young age and would do anything to get him back," my teacher said. Many students always say, "I just want to make my parents proud of me and proud of what I am doing." So losing a loved one changes their lives forever! However, most people do not realize that until it actually happens to them. Therefore, when students have certain things going on in their lives outside of school, and they have to worry about school and their grades, then they do not think the stuff they are learning now in school is going to help them in the future.

The second great reason for high school students' apathy towards mathematics and low performance on standardized tests is that students see mathematics as a subject irrelevant to their lives and future career plans. A grandmother of a West Aurora High School student said, "You have to use math everywhere you go. There is not one thing that does not involve math in your regular lives." Students complain all the time, saying we are never going to use these math methods again. This is wrong! There is going to be more technology that is new and other things that we will have to figure out. A parent of a student from West Aurora High School said, "They don't take it seriously because they don't think they will need it later in life. Math actually prepare students for college." Students end up messing around, getting off topic and not paying attention to the teacher in class. If they want to pass and move up to the next grade level, or even graduate high school, they are going to have to put effort into their work and class.

The third great reason for the high school students' apathy towards mathematics and low performance on standardized tests is that teachers teach math in boring ways. Students want a fun and entertaining teacher that can teach them how to solve math problems that they can actually enjoy and remember. A teacher from West Aurora High School said, "This apathy is not a school problem but a societal one. Schools can make education free and fair for all demographics; ensure that students are placed in proper classes, based on their previous performances; and, put support systems in place to assist students to achieve to their upmost potential."

Some students think it is the teacher. Another student from West Aurora High School said, "Teachers should make the class fun so it can catch students' attention. They should be better prepared to talk about the importance of mathematics, not just about the test." All that students want is that their teachers make their instruction more entertaining, something we can all enjoy. This school year, they have this new trivia game called Kahoot, which the teacher lets the students use their cellphones or one of the school's laptop. I heard that everyone loves to play; so, maybe they should play every day for about 10 minutes instead of once a month. This could help many students remember how to do certain problems and enjoy the class instead of sleeping and drooling all over the desk.

When I asked a couple of students what was their weakest and strongest subject in school, a lot of them said that math was their weakest because their teachers explained the problems but not clearly enough for them to understand. When they ask their teachers to explain how to solve the problem again, their teachers gave them an attitude. Then I asked the students, "What do you think the school can do? One student said, "They can have everyone take a standardized test based on their previous classes so it shows if they have improved." Another student said, "Giving everyone the same test is wrong because they are not taking in consideration that not every student has the same knowledge as a 'typical student.'" I asked myself, "What is a typical student?" I learned from the same two students that typical students are the ones who meet all the tests' benchmarks, meet all their teachers' requirements, get all their work done and have little to no problems understanding the content taught in class. These two students feel that, since they are not typical, they should not take the same test.

In conclusion, I learned through my research that the three greatest reasons for students' apathy towards mathematics and low performance on standardized tests are students' lack of time to put in the necessary effort; their belief that math is an irrelevant subject; and teachers' boring way of teaching. A lot of teachers and adults may feel that I am wrong; however, I know how students feel because I am a student myself.

Breianna Rodriguez

Throughout my years as a student, I have been enrolled in many math courses. My name is Breianna Rodriguez. I am a sixteen-year-old student that has felt the defeat and success of the mathematical language. Throughout this essay, I will explain the reasoning why American students dislike math and give some examples of ways to correct this issue. The point of this essay is not only to figure out why students do not like math but also to understand why they perform so poorly on standardized tests.

Math has been discovered and utilized by ancient societies for more than ten thousand years; and yet Americans still treat it as an enemy. Students dread the subject and when hit with difficulty, remarks such as, "We're never going to use this in our line of work," "Math is boring," or even "This is useless," begin to pour out. As these ideas crowd our classrooms, the opinions of students who love math begin to change. Mathematics is filled with thousands of complicated apparatuses that must come to an implicit or never-ending answer. Mathematics is the most unappreciated subject but the most important skill that is needed everywhere. If our generation understood the importance of learning mathematics, the future could be filled with a larger amount of well-educated doctors, police officers, accountants, bankers, and architects. Our country could be at the top of worldwide educational systems, instead of having eleven other countries ahead of us.

Why students accept low performance in mathematics? While talking to a former classmate, he explained his disinterest in math when he said, "A lot of the stuff we learn in math doesn't apply to jobs that appeal to what the younger generation is interested in." Although math can be difficult to understand, it is tough to find a job that does not have to do with math. Sure, there are jobs that only use basic arithmetic; however, what will be the income from those jobs? Will the job have a lasting position? What students do not understand is that, in order to live a remotely decent lifestyle, we will need a substantial large income. Society has not breeched these students' minds to think about the reality that there will bills and daily expenditures to pay. Even if students choose a career that only requires minimal math, there is little chance that they could have the career they enjoy because of how competitive the world is. Math-filled careers pay substantially more than the non-math filled. If our generation continue to believe math is useless, the future will be crowded with uneducated masses.

Their torpid and immature attitude and lack of effort in learning math will get them to become homeless.

After all, why not suck it up and push through the hardships to perform well in math? Being able to see the accomplished work that was completed with such ambition is usually worth the extensive, tedious and on occasion, repetitious homework. If students were a bit more meticulous with the assignments they turned in, and saw their grades at their optimum, then they would be captivated to transact their best every time. Mathematics can be problematic! It is very easy to fall behind but extremely difficult to catch up. However, nothing worth pursuing can be achieved without pain, mentally or physically.

When I learned that, in mathematics, students in the United States were outperformed by their peers from 11 other countries, I was raged! Demoralization and disappointment filled not only my mind but also my heart. It is so sad to learn that we could do better, but choose not to, because math is too difficult. After hearing this information, I knew why these statistics were true. I already knew that China, India and Japan would score higher than the United States. It is a no brainer. They study and take higher qualifying classes and practice before they practice. For example, before taking Algebra during the school year, they take Algebra during summer. They also work twice as hard in their free time, when American students are playing video games. We could do a lot better if we put in as much effort in math and science as we do in materialistic things. Students in the United States need a wakeup call. We need to leave our unrealistic world and begin to walk in the shoes of future scholars.

While preparing for a new school year, the schools throughout different districts can collaborate to find new and exciting ways to get our students intrigued. While interviewing a classmate, he expressed that, "The school officials need to teach us stuff that is more relevant to our lives and not from textbooks from the 70's and 80's." Not everyone will be excited about having new books, but having up-to-date examples and problems can provide a less repetitious classroom environment. When taking math in school, students begin to get sluggish and dis-attached. Although taking notes is helpful and needed, an alternative that can help students learn is math games. Teachers can also give students a challenge or a goal for the day. Taking notes day in and day out does not allow students to participate and interact with each other that much.

It can be very frustrating to catch up when students miss a class. There should be a certain class, or time during the day when the students can go for help. Having an alternate place to go to ask questions for further understanding can be efficient as well. Another thing that is important in the students' learning process is their relationship with their teachers. When first meeting the students, it is crucial that teachers make them feel like they can come to get help whenever needed. In a previous experience, I met with a teacher that was a bit intimidating. Although I was doing an okay work in my Geometry class, I was struggling. I refused to ask for help because I felt deficient; however, towards the beginning of the second semester, Mrs. Braves pulled me aside and told me to meet her at the study group she held. I went a little unsure. When I walked in, she was going over all the problems that students got the wrong answer on a quiz. I felt less intimidated and began to correct all the silly and sometimes lazy answers I gave on that quiz. I went to her study group almost every day for a year. I never in my life enjoyed math that much. Teachers reaching out, even when no one ask them to do so, can change students' perceptions about them and most importantly the class.

Having read the substantial amount of information and knowledge about why American kids hate math and have a poor performance in standardized tests, I have faith that minds will change. Although our country has failed in the past, who says that it is too late to change the minds of our students?

Dr. Lourdes Ferrer

Christian Ramirez

Before I get into the actual paper, let me introduce myself. My name is Christian Ramirez and I currently attend West Aurora High School. Throughout my four years here at the high school, I have taken different math courses, which I have enjoyed. However, there were times where I felt like giving up because I was not able to do a problem or simply because I was lazy. After High School is over this upcoming May, I am planning to enroll in college and earn a degree in Biochemistry, while meeting the pre-med requirements. After I earn my degree in Biochemistry, I plan to continue on to Medical school and specialize in Neurosurgery. I am anticipating this career will require a lot of Mathematics. What really got me to write this paper is that I, myself, have had apathy towards mathematics and have sometimes given up on my math classes. I have fellow friends that struggle and do not like math, and finally yet importantly, there are many people, including myself, that are very lazy. We give up too easily when we struggle. Though I can still have laziness in me, I try to keep it at a low or zero level. I came to realize that most of the careers that are competitive in the world right now require mathematics. In other words, we have to take higher-level math courses in college and cannot get away from them. At the end of the day, you commit to embracing the subject in spite of your feelings; it is the adult thing to do.

Many students take math courses not knowing what math means. Mathematics is an abstract science that includes numbers, quantities, shapes, the space, etc. Mathematics may be studied in its own right (pure mathematics) or as it is applied to other disciplines (applied mathematics) such as physics and engineering. A question that many students tend to ask is, "Why is math so important in life?" The answer to the question may vary; however, the answer that I want to give is that, if you want to earn a lot of money in your job, you will need to study a competitive degree. Did you know that most competitive degrees are likely to require students to take high-level math courses in college if you want to earn a lot of money? Some examples of jobs that require a lot of math and pay the most are engineering and anything in the sciences, including health sciences.

Well, it is time for the part that everyone is waiting for. The first reason why students have apathy towards math and low performance in standardized tests is their lack of interest. When I say lack of interest, I do not mean that they should love it. I think they should try even if they do not like it. For example, look at the Asian culture. I am sure that not all Asians have a passion for math; but they know math is a class that they have to take and that math will lead them to well-paying jobs in the future. In all honesty, when you try in a class that you claim you "hate," the class becomes a lot more interesting because you become more curious to see how it applies to real life. You just want to keep studying it in greater depth. Referring back to the Asian culture, you know how Asians are stereotyped. Is it that they are geniuses in math and science? Although Hispanics have a negative stereotype, we have the capability to change that; but it will require a lot of effort. A big reason for our low performance in standardized tests is that some students are unprepared to take the test. Some students do not have experience taking standardized tests. Overall, I am certain that if others can do it, we can do it as well. We are all capable of achieving the same things.

The second reason behind students' apathy towards mathematics and low standardized test scores is that it requires students to put a lot of work. Seeing so many students in my math class complaining about how hard the material is makes me upset. It bothers me that they give up too easily. A math problem can be very simple. However, if students see variables, something that they have never seen before, they give up by default. As students take higher-level math courses such as Calculus, they will find math to be more rigorous and problems to be longer and more difficult to solve. It gets to the point where math is a "foreign language" for too many students. I, myself, was like them not long ago. I thought math was pointless in my life. I would not even attempt to solve a problem that I thought I could not solve! However, honestly, let us be realistic. You master only the material that you practice. I had to get rid of my egotistical mindset that said, "I'm naturally good at math. I can catch on quickly." That behavior led me to no good; in fact, it brought my GPA down. I can only hope that this kind of attitude towards mathematics improves in every student's heart.

The third reason why students have apathy towards mathematics and have low standardized test scores is that not everyone wants to do something in life that involves math. I will start with myself. It was not until high school that I started to learn about different career options. Through most of my high school education, I wanted to be a doctor; but I never thought I had to take any math, just anatomy courses. Well, I was wrong! When I started to struggle in math, I started to pursue other careers that did not require too much math. I had always enjoyed courses such as biology and chemistry, but I did not want to take any other math course above calculus. I realized that, "There is not a science career that I enjoyed that did not require a strong math foundation." I decided to say to myself. "Suck it up and deal with it!" Because of that decision, I am firmly planted and I can now reach for the stars in my career goals.

Although many students have their excuses for not enjoying mathematics, it is not always their fault. Sometimes the students' teachers make the students get lost in class. Therefore, a teacher can do several things to help students. The first thing a teacher can do to improve the attitude of students towards math is to be passionate about the subject. For example, when I was in Algebra 2, my teacher was very passionate about everything she taught. Her being passionate about what she taught made me get interested in the class. Everything made sense and I was good at it. I have also had teachers who were not passionate about math. It is in those courses that I struggled the most and could not get involved. I realized that I could do well in any class that teachers showed passion for what they were teaching. When this is not the case, then it is a lot harder for me, and likely for other students, to be interested in the class. Therefore, it is not fully the students' fault when they lack interest in math. The teacher also factors in. One recommendation I will tell teachers is to simply be passionate and get involved with the students. It makes the students more interested and they learn better.

The second recommendation I will give teachers is to be more prepared for their lectures. Although teachers might know what they are teaching, it might not make sense to the students the way they are teaching it. For example, teachers should put themselves in the students' seat. They need to think if they would understand the content themselves. It has happened to me, and many of my friends. Explaining a rule and how to use it to solve a problem, and then using a different method to solve a similar problem, can confuse students. When the test comes, students have no idea which way to approach a problem. I am not saying that teachers are teaching wrong. I am saying that teachers should provide students with a better explanation about which method to use and why.

Well, it might seem like I am just on the students' side and against teachers; but students also have to put forth effort. Many students blame it on the teacher and all, but even if that was the case, students have many other resources. The internet, for example, can be very helpful if used properly. Students also have other teachers or tutors they can go to and they have friends who can help them understand the material. There should not be any excuse as to why students do not do well in their math classes. They have plenty of resources at their disposal. The best recommendation that I can give to students is to seek help if they need to.

In conclusion, as many statistics have shown, Hispanics and African Americans tend to have the lowest standardized test scores and it is mainly because of their lack of interest. That does not mean we are dumber than the rest; it just means that we lack preparation for those exams. It is my firm belief that we are capable of being at their same level or even higher. Only we, individually, can change that. We have to make ourselves more interested in the class, and if we do not like it, then we must suck it up and deal with it. It is not the last time you will take math. Can we imagine a world where minorities are not discriminated because of their lack of education? I definitely can. In several years, Hispanics will no longer be a minority. We will be the majority. We will feel accomplished when we see that most Hispanics are no longer at the bottom of ladder, instead at the top, where we are supposed to be.

Dr. Lourdes Ferrer

Crystal Magana

Math, a subject we are all told to take. Even though there is always that one student who loves it and makes it look easy, many do not see it that way. Students have low-test scores, specifically in math. I can relate to those who struggle in math. It used to be an easy subject for me in early school years. I would be excited about the very simple one-answer questions (back when letters were not involved). Math became more of a challenge when letters, graphs, Pi and decimals were added to solving problems. Even though I am only a junior in high school, math is not going to go away anytime soon. Therefore, learning how to deal with them and knowing why they are so important would improve my perspective regarding math. I am writing this paper because I know that I am not the only one who finds math challenging, at least most times. I also want to explain the reasons behind students' apathy towards mathematics and low performance on standardized tests.

Let me explain a little bit what math is all about. To begin, one must first understand why math is so important.

Although I always knew that math was important, once I began to research it, I realized that my assumptions were way off track. After doing some deep research, I learned that math helps students learn concepts in a more organized way, guides their cognitive development and clarifies understanding. Math is very important because it teaches communication, connection, and representation. Therefore, math teaches more than just subtracting and adding numbers. Math is a skill that we use in life.

I did not just stop by finding out what math is, I also thought about certain issues that can make students not try hard in mathematics. One reason was that many do not find it necessary for their future careers. I asked a couple of my peers why they did not like math and they replied with, "It is not important later on in life and people don't want to learn about something they don't like." I even heard a short story from a close friend in which she expressed her opinion. She began by telling me how she had a passion for make-up, hairstyles and nails. She wanted to study cosmetology. "I hate math. I do not like it. I also never understood half of what my teacher would teach in class. She was not even a bad teacher. I am simply not a math person. I actually want to take a class where I can do what I like and math is not one. I want to study cosmetology. I feel certain that if I study cosmetology and spend my life doing other peoples' hair and make-up, math would never interfere with that." What my friend needs to consider is that as a hair stylist, she must mix hair dye at the correct ratio. She must also manage the financial aspect of the business. A better grasp on math will provide her with the knowledge and understanding to run her very own business. You cannot escape math!

For a good while, I started to agree with her when she said, "I do need to find the value of 'x' or 'y' in this career!" What concerned me about her story was, "What if you change your mind and end up going into a math-related field?" I have noticed that many students perceive math as useless. The benefits and beauty of mathematics is practically impossible for many students to see.

There are many reasons for someone to justify students' hate towards mathematics. I spoke with an accountant who once hated math. She told me how she was terrible at math and never liked it. Like most of us, she never had the highest grade in her class. She also told me how she never tried in math because she did not know what she wanted her career to be. At the end, she made it clear to me. "You should always try because you can change your mind about what career you actually want to go into." She went into a career that uses many math skills. Most people convince themselves that unless they are dealing with large amounts of money, math is not really necessary. I know this should not continue to be an excuse for students to stop trying in math.

Another reason is that students have a hard time remembering what they learned in math. Math is like a foreign language. It has many symbols, rules and formulas that students must memorize. I can agree that there are many different ways to solve a problem, but the amount of possibilities can frustrate anyone! I have come across people that literally had to cheat their way out of tests. Some would write the formulas in their wrists, on the table, and even on water bottles. Others did not even try to do well. When I mentioned this to my cousin, she replied to me by saying, "Teachers only make the process harder."

I noticed that my math class was all memorization, but in my physics class, there were formula sheets. Regarding this, one of the people who I interviewed said, "Not all math-related classes include using formula sheets to help students out. It would be nice to have them in math." I always asked myself this until I realized that the ACT does not allow formula sheets. I learned that students lack well-developed mental strategies for remembering mathematic facts and algorithmic procedures. After learning this, I had a light bulb moment. I realized that teachers in high school almost never teach students how to memorize concepts in an easier way. Teachers believe that memorization is not that hard, especially since we are used to memorizing things all the time like phone numbers, addresses, classes, and names. Students should not find this to be a reason to despise math, just because it takes time, effort and practice to not only understand but to also memorize.

There is another reason, besides these two, that I feel is more delicate. Students fear saying the wrong answer in front of their peers. I always had this issue and to this day, I sometimes still do. Because I knew that I needed more than just my opinion, I decided to do an anonymous survey. I found out that students feel like they will be seen as a less intelligent people if they say the wrong answer. Many people believe that impressing their friends is too important to risk publicly giving the wrong answer. Saying the wrong answer can make them feel stupid or embarrassed. I read those answers many times because I knew that I could relate to them so much. I knew how much I love the compliments I get every time I answer correctly or get a good grade. However, when math became more challenging, I rarely raised my hand or asked a question. I would find every way possible to avoid answering or sharing my answer. I had a bad attitude towards math. It was like confronting my worst enemy. I was not aware that a positive attitude, diligence and hard work could lead to academic success. Although I wish I learned this before, I realized that I could still change my attitude. I knew that spending more time learning math was hard work. I still fear giving the wrong answer, and so do many people, even the top students. Nevertheless, there are ways we can all overcome this fear.

I sought teachers' recommendations to face this fear and many of their responses were pretty positive. One teacher told me to not fear giving the wrong answer because he also made mistakes in front of his students. He specified that, "learning math is about exploring and discovering." It convinced me; however, I still wanted to know how a teacher could encourage other students so they could also have a more positive attitude. A different math teacher told me, "I would encourage students and tell them that it's okay to be wrong. Since a math class is a learning environment, it is okay to make mistakes." Then it came to me! Teachers do not clarify enough that school is a learning environment. We should let students know that learning and making mistakes is not a bad thing. That way they can be far more comfortable to answer questions, even if they are wrong.

To conclude, I convinced myself that these are just three out of many more reasons why students perform low in standardized tests and do not enjoy their math classes. It is important to understand that there are many students who are giving up for reasons like these or similar and do not realize that there are solutions. There are people who can encourage students to have a positive attitude towards mathematics! If you are student, I hope that after all these examples you are inspired to actually try!

Fernanda Valencia

I am a person who is easily influenced because I do not have strong opinions. I fail a lot before I succeed and I am never really sure if the final decisions I made were right. All throughout my elementary and middle school education, math and music have been the two things that I have excelled at the most. I understand that it sounds nerdy and geeky but I have my reasons. In math, it does not matter how you get the answer. The only thing that is truly important is the product, the final result. I never completely hated math. I did dislike many aspects of it; but I never understood why so many people disliked it to the point where they hated it. It was until I met Dr. Lourdes and she asked us a simple question, "What is so bad about math?" Dr. Lourdes encouraged me to find the answer to that question. After conducting a series of interviews and researching online, I found out that the three greatest reasons for high school students' apathy towards mathematics and low performance on standardized tests are that students do not have the discipline to think hard enough to solve math problems. They just quit! Another reason is that students fear saying the wrong answer in front of their peers. That is why they would rather stay quiet and not say anything. Students also see mathematics as a subject irrelevant to their lives and future career plans.

Before I go more into depth regarding the reasons for students' apathy towards mathematics, I would like to go over what mathematics actually is. Math the abstract science of number, quantity, and space. Nevertheless, this simple definition can be applied to a myriad of things like physics, chemistry, engineering, etc. Math is definitely crucial in the adult life.

Now that I have shared a little, we can go into the first reason with more understanding. The first reason for high school students' apathetic behaviors towards mathematics is that we do not have the discipline to think hard enough to solve math problems. If we reflect on times before technology eased our daily lives, we had to memorize and solve an infinite amount of things for ourselves. We had to memorize telephone numbers, presidents, state capitals, the periodic table of the elements and the multiplication tables. We were required to use maps to find our way and go shopping. Our generation has lost the ability to think, memorize and concentrate. In our era, everything can be solved with a GPS, a calculator or with internet access. Since we no longer have the discipline or thrive to solve things for ourselves, it is easy to give up when a problem arises that cannot be solved with an electronic device.

Mathematics is a subject that requires time, concentration and memorization. Reyna, a student I interviewed, said, "It is so much easier to take out my phone and google the formulas. No one wants to think that much." She is right. Most students attempt a problem but do not have the domestication to try until they have reached a correct conclusion.

There are multiple ways to solve problems, mathematical and real life ones. One way to develop the discipline we need to solve math problems is to rely less on our loved technology and choose to think on our own. If we manage to somehow train and discipline ourselves to memorize and concentrate more, we can hopefully by default, change the way we deal with many things, math being one of them. Concentrating to the point where we finish what we start, would be amazing growth. Even something as small as completely cleaning your room and not doing anything else until you finish would be great progress. Trust me, as a sixteen-year-old girl, I know all about distractions. We are surrounded by distractions such as Netflix, social media networks, and even sleep; anything but finishing the tasks, we already have in progress. Starting and finishing a complex math problem that is hard to understand is frustrating and in many ways discouraging; but maybe, turning it into a task that we can complete could help us develop the discipline we need to do well in math.

Another reason for the disinterest in mathematics appears to be the fear students have about giving an incorrect statement in front of their fellow classmates. No one takes pleasure in being incorrect, especially in front of people who they know. Since there are so many ways to make mistakes in math, people have a gargantuan probability in making an error. The problem is that no one is willing to ask questions. I have heard fellow peers say, "How do you even get this?" One day in my math class, a very quiet girl said to me, "I'm always wrong! I don't even know why I'm in this class." However, I have never heard her ask a question. Everyone thinks fondly of the idea of equality; but since we are so focused on not feeling inferior to others, we trade the improvement of our education for the hope that we do not look shortsighted in front of our friends and colleagues.

Honestly, some of the ways to remove this problem would be to get our priorities straight. Before I began to research this, I have noticed that I myself had my priorities messed up. I thought that people were going to think less of me because I needed assistance in understanding a certain math problem; however, when I dare to ask my peers would thank me. They had the same question but did not dare to ask. They were so worried about what others thought that they put their education in jeopardy.

There are some people who actually like math; but since it is socially acceptable to dislike it, they say, "I hate it too!" People who like mathematics are viewed as nerds in our society and that is not how students want to be viewed. The focus we put on what others think must decrease and the focus that we put on our education should increase. Teachers could also help by asking for students' involvement and motivating their pupils to ask more questions. I have heard of teachers handing out candy to participating students, rewarding them for to their engagement.

Students see mathematics as a subject irrelevant to their lives and future career plans. "Students see little pieces of math but don't see the big picture. They don't know where math applies in the real world," stated Mr. Feigle. When we do not think we are going to use information, we disregard it and do not think anything of it. We remember information that we are probable to use in the future. High school students do not necessarily see how the Pythagorean Theorem is going to help them in life, especially when the field they want to go into is something like psychology or social work.

A recommendation to fix this would be to ask teachers to help students see the relevance of math and how it applies to real life situations. I find it helpful when teachers tell stories about how they used math to solve problems, like when they know how to choose a cable or phone company in the most frugal way.

There are things everyone needs to do in order to make students' apathy towards math decrease. Teachers could try to be more energetic and lively while teaching. They can also try to use more real life problems for students to solve with mathematics so that high school students can see its relevance. Parents can try to encourage their children to believe in themselves. I strongly feel that students are the ones who most change the most. We, as students, need to understand that there will always be situations in which we want to give up and challenges where we may think that there is no solution; but mathematics, as dorky as it may sound, is amazing! It gives us hope that there is a right answer to every problem and even though it is hard, we can get through it. When we put our priorities in order and establish that our education is more important than whatever others may think of us, then we can become better learners. I know that mathematics is a hard, challenging and tedious subject, but as Dr. Lourdes always says, "We need to suck it up and deal with it!"

Gerardo Caballero

My name is Gerardo Caballero and through my short years of life, I have not experienced everything, but I have enough experience to know some of the greatest flaws the world faces today. Without a doubt, I see education as the resolution to any problem. Exceedingly important, each new generation of children must realize the importance of education, especially their mathematical studies to reach success in school and in life. Through the light of my own experience and research, I plan to reveal the reality that America faces today; many students have grown apathetic towards standardized tests, especially in the subject of mathematics. After conducting a series of informal interviews and researching online, I found out reasons for high school students' apathy toward mathematics and low performances on standardized. The three greatest reasons are students' irrational fear to ask questions or seek help, students' upbringing, and students' doubt regarding the importance of mathematics.

Mathematics makes itself present in every aspect of our life from money, to technology, and medicine. Mathematics is defined as the systematic treatment of magnitude, relationship between figures and forms, and relationships between quantities expressed symbolically. Mathematics was discovered at the beginning of recorded history. Prehistoric societies used mathematics no more than for counting and keeping track of time, and seasons using the sun. Most mathematical discoveries did not appear over night; thanks to the work of our mathematical ancestors and civilized societies, math has evolved from a tiny droplet into an ever-flowing stream that grants life to the forms around it. Even though one may see our calumniating knowledge of mathematics as a mathematical Golden Age, the real improvements and progress of mathematics are yet to come. As a society, we may feel at such peace, harmony, and stability that we have begun to rely exceedingly on computers, calculators, and smartphones to aid us in the most simplistic arithmetical situations; forgetting the benefit, beauty, and resourcefulness of mathematics. In the Era of Information, the importance of Mathematics exceedingly highlights every part of each new generation's life. Mathematics also improves children's employability since most high in demand and high paying jobs demand a strong foundation in math and science. Practicing math strengthens the mental muscles essential to build stamina and agility to solve problems not only in math, but also in life. The practice of mathematics may also save money and time in college in the way that if students achieve a score higher than 21 in the math portion of the ACT, they avoid having to take prep-math courses during their college first year.

Initially, as high school students' apathy towards mathematics increases, their performance on standardized tests decreases. According to my research, 75 percent of students, math teachers and the public believe that students' upbringing influences not only their mathematical performance, but also their academic lives in general. In many socioeconomic disadvantaged households including broken families, homeless families, minorities' families, among other possibilities, their children's education might not be a priority. In these situations, parent's largest concerns can include supporting their families, surfacing from economic instability, language barriers, and conforming to the American lifestyle instead of their children's education. These households often lack interest, because either the academic content is unfamiliar to the parents or there is a language barrier forming between parent and child. It affects their children's academic career and mathematic performance.

My Algebra 2 teacher ponders about her two-year-old nephew, how he wakes up every morning with such excitement and desire to go to school. She concludes that students initially have great enthusiasm and enjoyment for school in their Elementary School years, and that enthusiasm slowly declines. The effects of such change makes itself present in the Middle School and High School years when Algebra makes its appearance. If parents do not instill positive learning habits to their children and keep their rigor going, their children will not develop the responsibility, smart-hard work ethic, persistence, and the ability to delay gratification, necessary to perform well in school, especially in mathematics. Thus, despite the adversities a family may encounter, parents' attitudes and involvement in their children's life will affect their academic and level of math proficiency. Such involvement and positive behaviors toward mathematics and school in general hold importance because learning mathematics requires persistence, discipline, and confidence. In order to excel in math, students need all these characteristics, which are only learned at home and strengthened by parents.

High school students' apathy towards mathematics and low performance on standardized tests alarm parents, teachers, students, and the nation, however, what reasons hide behind the truth? Students perceive mathematics as a subject irrelevant to their lives and future career plans. This kind of mentality ultimately leads to students' downfall in mathematics. Many of the students interviewed live by the classical whine, "When am I ever going to use this?" when referring to mathematics. These students are oblivious about what math can offer them. Students may not perceive mathematics as important because their teacher may not emphasize its importance. It is not enough for teachers to assign, collect, and grade homework. Teachers must let students know the importance of the assignment, and how it conveys to their everyday life, in order to help students appreciate and realize the importance of math in their lives and future career.

Students have also become victims to the societal belief that mathematics is virtually inexistent beyond high school. When in reality, most high in demand and high paying careers demand a strong foundation in mathematics and science. With the limited competent spots in careers, future employers seek individuals with well-developed mental strategies and other notable characteristics commonly attained from math, especially the ability to use logic! If students are good at math, most likely they are good problem solver, a characteristic vital for children's employability in the future. To flourish in any field, mathematics requires students' undivided attention and appreciation. Therefore, because mathematics prepares students mentally and mathematically, it should not be perceived as useless. Students need to make an effort to understand its foundation; otherwise, it is practically impossible for them to see its beauty and applicability. Once students understand math, they are likely to like it or at least have a sense of satisfaction knowing math proficiency can help them graduate college debt- free with a high in demand degree.

The mathematical skills and abilities of American students have significantly begun to diminish. Amongst the myriad of explanations why is that they do not ask questions. Paula, a person who works as an assistant at high school discipline office, extensively works with students going through academic issues. Several students expressed to her that their teachers talk, and talk, and talk nonstop. At the end of the day, students feel like they were taught in a foreign language, with a lexicon that include words such as algorithms, reciprocals, math sequences, etc. Mathematics, for many students, does not sound like English. Despite needing help, students keep quiet because they fear their instructors or peers' reactions. Therefore, students' fear and anxiety to reach for assistance becomes a psychological impediment that hurts students' performance in math and standardized tests in general. Students also act passively in the classroom to circumvent many actions and feelings including menacing-like reprimands from their teachers and parents, and feelings of inferiority compared to the students who grasp the material at a faster pace. If students cannot build enough courage to ask questions and ask for assistance, their situation will not get better. Many students have a delusional idea that they can run away from their problems by ignoring them and keeping them secret; however, the grim reality is that problems fester into excruciating painful outcomes when left untreated. Students must not feel shame for not knowing everything! Academic triumph is the end result of students' desire to learn and ability to overcome fear and ask questions.

As students' apathetical views toward mathematics increases and their performance on standardized test decreases, the importance for recommendations to solve these problems grows. If students work with each other to learn, they will reach greater success. Recently, the science department in West Aurora High School organized a study night at Luigi's Pizza and Fun Center to prepare for the science finals. Students, not only had the opportunity to ask teachers and friends science questions, but also socialize and have fun; a vital part in the learning process.

Another example of how the teamwork of friends and classmates empowers students can be seen with the group of writers from *Grooming for Excellence* Student Leadership Academy. We have built such a strong bond that we confide on each other for help and encouragement during the difficulty process of writing this essay. Therefore, a useful recommendation for students would be to adopt friendly relationships with their classmates. These relationships allow students to help each other in times of trouble. Friends can be great study partners. A friend can encourage you through difficult moments communicate with you via technology in case you have a question. The goal is to persevere academically, especially in challenging subject such as mathematics.

To ameliorate the situation of students, proposals need to be considered or else students' low performance in mathematics will only increase. A point to be considered is a stronger relationship between parents, teachers, and students. The relationship between these three parties can be described as a triangle. Since a triangle is composed of three sides, without their connections with each other the triangle would not exist. If the student is not willing to do his part, the teacher and the parents' contributions will be in vain. If the parents do not do their part, a disconnection is created between the student and his teacher. If the teacher is not willing to help, there is little that the students and parents can do. Therefore, the participation of the three parties is an integral part in the academic field. The full attention and participation of parents, teachers and students is necessary to be successful in math.

Once identified that students feel apathetical towards mathematics and their performance on standardized test decreases, action needs to be taken in this instant to solve the problem. A possibility that might help students and instructors might include teachers taking a different teaching approach. Because teachers tend to deliver mathematics in a way that mostly benefits auditory learners, students with other learning styles shutdown, do not participate, and do not understand. Auditory learners, for example, learn best through the recital of information. Visual learners comprehend information presented to them in the forms of graphics and demonstrations. Kinesthetic learners can better benefit from hands-on methods such as tactual activities and experiments. One time in one of *Grooming for Excellence* seminars, Dr. Lourdes challenged students to make a right triangle, but not on paper! She challenged students to build a right triangle using their hands, arms, and bodies. Initially, students faced confusion, since they have never taken this kind of approach, but with some assistance, the students succeeded in building a right triangle. The kids from the *Grooming for Excellence* academy will never forget this experience because they never experienced a completely different approach. Not everyone has the same innate learning style. In order for a student to become more flexible, they must practice using a combination of learning styles. Therefore, teachers must combine learning tactics that benefit not one, but every type of student. That way the student not only benefits from their dominant learning style, but also practices perfecting their submissive learning styles to aid their academic performance.

In conclusion, after extensive research from informal interviews and online sources I have concluded that the three greatest reasons for high school students' apathetical views toward mathematics and low performances on standardized test are their doubt on the importance of mathematics, students' upbringing, and their irrational fear to ask questions and seek help. Mathematics is necessary, and until students learn the foundations of mathematics, they will not be able to see the applicability and beauty of this subject. Mathematics is a tool that can be used to tackle the greatest problems the world faces today. Students only need inspiration, persistence, and courageousness to make their wildest dreams come true. This essay was made possible through the collaboration between parents, teachers, students, and members of the community.

Gerardo Gonzalez

Many students across the country just absolutely hate math with a fire-burning passion. I used to be among those students who strongly disliked math, eventually I grew to love it. My name is Gerardo Gonzalez. I am currently a junior at West Aurora High School. When I was younger, I used to be good in math. Things changed when I went to middle school. I really struggled! During my first year in high school, I absolutely disliked algebra 1, but began to enjoy it a lot more during my second semester. During my sophomore year, I once again disliked geometry, partly because the teacher did not teach with the same passion as my former Algebra 1 teacher. However, now that I am a junior, I am fortunate enough to have the same teacher I had as a freshman, when I was taking Algebra 1. I can honestly say that I am absolutely enjoying math because of my teacher. I know as a fact that teachers can really make a difference in how much students appreciate mathematics.

Let me get straight to the point of this essay and write less about me. It is no secret that math is highly disliked by many students, but why? That is the focus of this essay. I decided to become part of a dedicated group of writers who want to help students who detest math and perform low on standardized testing. Writing this paper gives me a chance to help other students, and even parents and teachers, solve the tension that exists between mathematics and students. After conducting a series of interviews and researching online, I found that the three greatest reasons for students' apathy towards math and low performance on standardized tests are that students do not see the connection between math and the real world; do not put in the time needed to grasp math concepts and pick the easy way out. Although many reasons exist for this problem, these are the ones I found more common. Now, I will proceed to tell you a bit of the history behind this godly science that we learned is math.

Since the beginning of time, people have felt that need to organize, whether it was cattle or cornstalks. When history began to be recorded, The Mayans, The Chinese, the people of the Indus valley, The Egyptians, and the people of Mesopotamia between the Tigris and the Euphrates River, had all developed impressive amounts of mathematical concepts. Proof of this can be found in documents from Egypt that date back to 1900B.C. Egyptians used algebra in order to calculate the volume of the pyramids they so gracefully constructed. The Mesopotamians utilized mathematics in cuneiform writings on clay tablets, which date all the way back to 2100B.C. They created the number system base of 60, which has been preserved to this day, in our measuring of time. Also found on these tablets were multiplication tables, reciprocal tables, squares, and square roots. The mathematics in India involved the use of negative and even irrational numbers. India holds the credit for the development of the concept of zero, which evolved into current western mathematics and plays an important role as a placeholder in our current decimal number system. Thanks India! The Mayan civilization also developed the concept of zero. They were inspired by astronomy to develop mathematics. The concept of geometry sprouted in ancient Greece. Calculus developed during the 18th century; from then to now, modern mathematics developed.

The first reason for students' apathy is their attitude, meaning the way that they feel about the subject. For example, my first interviewee expressed that she did like math herself. She clarified that the reason why she dislikes it so much is simply because she is deficient in it. According to her, "Math either really clicks for some people or just not at all.". If this is true, then students think that there is no way out if they struggle in their math classes. I believe the students' attitudes are based on how much they can succeed in math. Take my interviewee for example. She disliked math since she was in high school and now that she is sophomore in college, she dislikes it even more. Why? She has that mindset that she is not skilled in math; therefore, she has a negative attitude towards mathematics.

A second common reason for students' apathy is that mathematics requires practice. The problem is, many students do not put in the required effort and they end up falling behind. Students often know that math is extremely difficult, but do not apply themselves because they are intimidated by the level of difficulty. Math is a step-by-step process and according to Elvira, "If one mistake is made, then everything is thrown off and people have a hard time finding the mistake." At times, students make mistakes due to lack of practice. Say for example, you have two students, Ty and Rich. Ty does his homework on a daily basis, while Rich rarely completes his homework. As you would expect, the student with the most practice was significantly more successful, because as people say, "Practice makes perfect!"

The final most common reason for apathy is the urge to pick the easy way out, for example, use calculators. A calculator is either a student's aid, or his worst enemy. Many students overuse calculators and rely on them for even the simplest problems. As Laura said, "Students don't feel the need to learn the processes behind mathematical computations." Imagine one student using a calculator to figure out that 100×2-100=100 and another simply braking it down as $100 \times 2 = 200$ and $200 - 100 = 100$. The second student actually did the steps and understood how to get the answer while the other had no thought behind the process. Laura also pointed out that, "Calculators do not let students focus on mathematical procedures."

An excellent solution to this commonly reoccurring problem is to take students to college campuses at a young age. By doing this, the students will feel a desire to succeed academically because according to Dr. Hiscock, current principal at West Aurora High School, "Some students don't see themselves as being able to succeed academically." Exposing students to colleges at an early age will give them the ambition that will motivate them to succeed academically. This would entirely solve the apathy that some students feel towards school in general, including math.

One thing that teachers can do is to encourage their students, rather than just teaching. Teachers should make math more enjoyable not only for the students but for themselves as well. Some of the teachers that I have encountered will immediately yell at students for making a mistake, which only feeds students' fear of math. Teachers must teach students that it is okay to make mistakes, but keep on practicing until they improve. This is extremely crucial because, early in life, students need to develop discipline to face challenges; so later on, they can face the challenges of post-secondary courses.

Colleges should reward those students with superb grades, which can inspire students to give their best. The colleges should offer rewards to students who earn high scores on the math portion of standardized tests as well as a high GPA. An example of this could be providing students 2 years of free education at state universities or community colleges. Laura, one of my interviewees, told me how in Arkansas, if high school seniors graduate with a cumulative GPA of at least 3.5, they receive 2 years of free college education at any college within the state. Students would definitely have that extra motivation to succeed if programs like this existed here in Illinois.

Now that I have shared with you the reasons behind and solutions to students' apathy towards mathematics and poor performance on math standardized testing, it is up to us to change our future as well as the future of others after us. It is a shame to see that other countries are beating us mathematically and overall academically. It is unacceptable. This must end now!

Jennifer Aguilar

My name is Jennifer Aguilar. I am currently a junior at West Aurora High School, and have exceeded the expectations of many people. I am a member of *Future Health Professionals (HOSA), Future Educators of Association (FEA), National Spanish Honor Society (NSHS), National Honor Society (NHS), Blackhawk Leadership Team (BLT),* a *Varsity Scholar Athlete* and an AP student. Surprising to some people, I am also Hispanic. Although born in the United States, the Hispanic culture has been a strong influence in my life because of my parents. My parents value education; they have influenced me to be an ambitious student.

Today, I am interested in being an Early Child Education teacher, specifically for bilingual children. In my opinion, it is the best field because early education is critical for young brains and Hispanics, on average, have perform low academically compared to the Caucasians and Asians. In theory, most Hispanics do poorly because of their language barrier; but mathematics is a universal language. Therefore, there must other reasons behind their low performance in math. To seek answers about racial differences in academic performances, I conducted several informal interviews with high school students, adults, and teachers, as well as obtained information from research studies. I interviewed widely affected Hispanic high school students. However, in order to obtain accurate research, I also interviewed math teachers and adults.

Math is an international language that has been used for centuries and will continue to be used. Math has been used to construct ancient Greek architecture, Galileo's inventions, Kepler's ellipse orbit of the planets, as well as today's synthetic drugs. Mathematics is not only important in universal discoveries but it is also used in everyday tasks like grocery shopping. In spite of this, the sad truth is that many students hate math and this apathy increases with each generation. Hispanic students do not have an encouraging home environment, find mathematics very difficult, and they lack effort.

Hispanics usually lack a home environment that is conducive to learning math. An encouraging environment is one in which students get support and recognition for their achievements. According to my survey, 75% of high school students believe that Caucasians and Asians outperform Hispanics and African Americans because they enjoy a positive learning environment. A Hispanic classmate shared with me a personal story when he was in third grade. He said that the whole class took their last math test of the year. Every student, except him, did a fabulous job on the test. His teacher announced that he received a C-minus when the rest of the class received an A. Since then, his peers mocked him constantly, saying things like, "You're dumb!" "You're an idiot!" and "Why do you even try?" He shared what occurred with his mother and she said, "It doesn't matter. Elementary school isn't important." So from then on, he felt worthless and never wanted to try again. Eight years later, he dropped out of high school. Now he works full time to help support his single mother and little sister. For the purpose of this research, I contacted him to ask, "What do you think could had helped you finish high school?" His response was, "My mother and teachers did not encourage me to stay in school. My mother asked me to drop out and work. No one had faith in me." Others like him have parents telling them that it is okay to be bad in math because they were bad too. Students need a positive influence in their lives in order to succeed academically. Sadly, many Hispanic parents do not expect much from their children.

In addition to Hispanic students not having and encouraging environment, they also find mathematics difficult. Gathered from my research, 100% of math teachers mentioned that Hispanic students' think math is too difficult. A high school

Pre-Calculus teacher said, "Every mathematic skill, study method, and formula is a brick, and the student is the cement that holds them together by applying them. If there is a missing piece in the structure, the entire building will crumble." Moving more into depth, my Algebra II teacher said, "If a student does not understand the material, ignores it, and never asks the teacher to slow down or for help, he will never understand the material." Another Algebra II teacher said, "The students who never fully understand the material and move on are the ones that struggle and they are the ones who hate math." Many teachers said that students ignore past math lessons because they see them as irrelevant. Since all seems irrelevant, they do not ask questions. Thus making mathematics more challenging as the years go on.

In addition to Hispanic students finding math too difficult, they also do not put in the necessary effort. I learned through my interviews that 80% of adults believe that many students find math boring, thus putting no effort into their work. Many confessed that they dread math class because it was too boring and long. One student shared that her brother would hate his math class because his teacher just gave students bookwork or worksheets, without teaching a lesson. They were expected to understand the content by themselves. It is for this reason that he is apathetic towards math and school in general.

Knowing now the main causes for Hispanic high school students' apathy towards mathematics, we must decide what to do to create the necessary change. To improve students' negative home environments, we have to change the community. School districts should host workshops where parents can learn basic math skills so they can help their children. Workshops on basic math skills are needed for Hispanic parents because many of them never attended proper schooling. Basic math knowledge would benefit the student and the parent. It would also encourage their children, as early as kindergarten, to pursue a college education. A workshop like this could also show parents that, in order to be a good student, their children must develop self-discipline. A child's early academic development will have a big impact later on in his life, once he becomes an adult. These workshops could teach everyone how to collaborate efficiently in order to eliminate Hispanic students' apathy towards mathematics.

In addition to providing a positive environment, making mathematics less difficult could also help Hispanic students feel less apathetic towards math. The saying practice makes perfect, is partially true. Efficient practice makes perfect and homework is practice. However, what good does it do if the student does not understand the material? As a suggestion, homework should be given but with a minimum of five minutes to start in class. This way the students can ask questions. Math homework should also contain real life math problem so the equations or formulas they use become relevant and useful in real life. Another way to make mathematics less challenging is to offer flexible tutoring hours for individuals as needed. Tutoring is provided in public schools, however many students cannot participate during those hours. Tutoring before and after school hours could benefit many students.

As well as making math less difficult, another way to reduce students' apathy towards mathematics is by making math more exciting. Hands on activities is always a great way to have students participate. However, the use of electronics seems to engage students, and there are several teaching apps that could help students understand the content and have fun at the same time. For example, *Kahoot*, *Khan Academy*, and *CoolMath4Kids*, all engage students and sometimes even gets them have fun.

In conclusion, Hispanic students have low performances on standardized tests and feel apathetic towards mathematics because they lack a positive environment, find mathematics difficult and do not put in effective effort. In my past, I have met several teachers who care about their students, their performances and their futures. If we continue being role models in our schools and everyone around us, we can annihilate the racial differences in academic performances.

I hope that in the future, every student will learn to appreciate mathematics.

Dr. Lourdes Ferrer

Jennifer Carrillo

In a minor study project that I conducted, which included vigorous hours of online research and individual interviews, I found that the three greatest reasons for high school students' apathy towards mathematics, and low performance on standardized test. Students do not take these tests seriously; they lack interest and motivation to achieve a great future; and, are overly praised by their teachers and schools.

Before I begin shearing with you the reasons why there is such a large amount of apathy towards math, I would like to explain what mathematics is. Mathematics is the science that deals with the logic of shape, quantity and arrangement. Math is something that we are surrounded by in our everyday lives, whether you we realize it or not. The study, practice and use of mathematics can be dated back into early civilizations. Starting with the Sumerians, which where the first people to develop a counting system, roughly in the year 2000 B.C. Many branches have grown from this simple system such as geometry, calculus, and algebra. Life without mathematics would be horrid; we would not have buildings, because architecture is all math, numbers, and angles. We could not even build a hut without some basic understanding of the mathematics behind structures. However, to those who love math, such as Dr. Lourdes Ferrer, math is a "divine science with a celestial language," that only a few passionate people can truly come to understand and love.

The first reason for students' huge apathy towards math and their low performance in standardized tests is that students do not take these tests seriously. During an interview that I was having with my friend Alex, who graduated high school and is now in college, he said that during testing, his friends would go to school under the influence of substances. I asked him, "Why would they do such a thing, knowing that these tests could have such a big on their lives?" He answered, "They could care less about their grades because they believe their parents will support them." Students are not taking these tests seriously because they think that they have their parents' support until they die. No one talks to them about their future; therefore, their future is not something they even think about. Student simply do not care about these tests. During an interview, I asked a friend how he felt about standardized tests. My friend looked at me, in the eyes, and said, "These test are stupid, they can't tell whether I am smart or dumb. They don't mean anything to me." My friend is the type of students that when we have a mandatory state test, she stays at home and sleeps in. Unfortunately, she truly believes that these tests have nothing to do with her placement in college and no impact on her life.

The second greatest reason why there is such apathy and low-test scores in standardized tests is the lack of interest and motivation for a better future. I was blessed to have parents and teachers who always had my back all the way through high school. I asked my mother Graciela, "Why do you think there is so much apathy towards math? "Why is it that Caucasian and Asian students perform better that Hispanics in standardized tests?" Her response was very straightforward. She said, "The reason is that in those ethnic groups education is largely praised. Hispanics do not value education as much as they do." Hispanics would rather start working in hard jobs that pay minimum salaries than working hard in getting a good education, so later on they can get a good job and live a better life." They rather start working the second they hit 16 and forget about school. The other races appreciate and praise education over work. While demonstrating a chart to one of my teachers, she pointed out that the reason for those results was that, "The culture of Whites and Asians value education more and consider it very important." The individual's needs of a student, for example, is more important than the immediate needs of the family unit. The reason there is such a performance gap between races is essentially the motivation to have a better future and the way they raise their children. For the sake of our future and our nation, this must change!

The final reason for apathy and low performance is that high school students believe that standardized tests are overly emphasized or praised. When you are in your teen years, you think that doing the opposite of what you are told to do is cool. It helps you fit in. That is exactly what is happening with these tests. The standardized tests that students are taking now are being presented to them as a big thing that you must do well. A student from my high school says that, "I hate walking into my counselor's office because all the posters she has hanging up are about the ACT". She feels like if she does poorly she has no future. Therefore, when the time to actually take the test comes, they have like a thousand pounds sitting on their shoulders. A former high school student said, "When I was taking the test, I swear, I could hear my teacher's voice telling me that I have to do well on this in order to have a good future." He said, "I could have done better if this test was not presented as a life or death situation." Another teacher said that, before the test, she likes to give her students a small pep talk to get them to relax; that they know what is on the test and everything is going to be okay. Every teacher should do this. If these standardized tests were less emphasized, students would take them with greater confidence and not overthink their choices.

Now that we know the three reasons for apathy and low performances, I will share with you some strategies to make things better. We can start with things we can do in the classroom. I know that I do better in math when I am noticed for my good job on a test. Luckily, at West Aurora High School, I have had a lot of luck with my math teachers. Mrs. Cirrincione and Mrs. Roberts are by far the best math teachers I have had. They know how to seat people so that those who talk to each other and create distractions sit nowhere near each other. These teachers are constantly stopping and asking us whether we have questions or not, and they teach with such enthusiasm that they set the mood to inspire students to want to learn. If every math teacher taught in this form, we would not have to be writing on how to make the apathy towards math shrink. The apathy towards math starts in the classrooms. If you have teachers who are willing to help each student, starting with a smile on their faces, everyone would be open to ask questions. If you have the unfortunate luck to have a teacher who does not approves questions, then you would not ask questions and easily be left behind. Considering that everything you learn in math now builds on the last thing you learned, not asking questions in a math class is a real bad thing.

My second recommendation is to start talking about the importance or mathematics at a very young age. Parents play such a large role in their children's future! If they let their children know that they must do well in school in order to have the life they want, then their children will have that idea engraved in their minds for the rest of their lives. Children need to know that they must "study there eyebrows off," as my parents always say. If you are taught math at a young age, you will understand what is going on in your current math class.

Parents must take time to sit down and essentially be a teacher for their children. They must sit down and teach their children basic arithmetic. I remember my mom before leaving to work telling us what multiplication table we had to write down fifty times by the time she got home. She did this during the summer. I remember hating her guts for doing that, but to this day, I thank her for being so strict on my siblings and me in math. Why? Because by the time I was in fifth grade, I knew all my multiplication tables like the back of my hand. Because of that, math is by far my favorite subject. I want to pursue a degree in math field. Therefore, if we want things to change for the better, parents must be the starting blocks to improve attitudes and test scores.

The last recommendation is that schools implement a different approach to educating students about testing. Someone that I interviewed told me that students know they are being compared to other people, which means that it is not about measuring their personal growth and progress. It is more about how they measure against their peers. They feel that they want to be accepted for who they are and can do. They do not like the fact that if you do not receive certain score, then you will be looked down upon. Unfortunately, some people simply cannot take a test even if their life depended on it. Then, there are those lucky ones who seem to know nothing, but are lucky enough to guess the right bubble to fill in. Tests are stressed so much that students think that their future solely depends on their scores. Nothing else matters! When in reality, it is not. Colleges also look at students' GPA. Students, who think that earning amazing ACT scores is all they need to be accepted in college, are incredibly wrong! Schools need to take time to correct these idiotic thoughts. High schools need to find better ways for helping students understand the reality of standardized tests.

I hope that these recommendations may help us all minimize students' apathy towards math and improve their performance on standardized tests for the sake of our country. We need more American doctors and engineers. We should not have to go all across the world to find them. This apathy towards math is foolish and unnecessary. If we learn to hate something, we should have the will power to turn that hate around and make it a positive feeling.

Dr. Lourdes Ferrer

Juan Martinez

Although I am only a high school student, I am going to explain to you why students hate mathematics. My team and I have gathered data from students, parents, and teachers on their thoughts about the topic. I have been in classrooms and have personally witnessed the tension in math classes. Although I like mathematics, I was curious on why other students hate mathematics. After conducting a series of informal interviews and researching online, I found out that the three greatest reasons for high school students' apathy towards mathematics and low performance on standardized tests are that students do not care and believe that math is not important. According to Emma, a sophomore at West Aurora High School, "Students who are not interested in the material will not put in their best effort." Rolando Orama, senior vice president of a well-known insurance company and father of two young girls, states that, "The parents at home need to be involved. The student's parents need to value mathematics." Rolando utilizes mathematics in his profession. If the parents value mathematics, it is likely that they will show their students the importance of mathematics. Kelly Vernon, an elementary school teacher, deals with this almost on a daily basis. She has been working with students for many years and says, "Technological tools do the math for you causing students to not do the math themselves." Students are taking the easier way of learning mathematics, which is affecting them in a way that most people do not realize. Students are not learning mathematics in a way that will make them remember the materials.

Mathematics is a science of numbers. Mathematics is used to solve any situation that you may encounter or come across. For example, mathematics can range from something as simple as a trip to the grocery store to an architectural plan for a skyscraper. Mathematics is needed on a daily basis, almost every minute of your life. Without mathematics, scientist would not be able to continue to discover new things that will benefit all of us. Everything would be so much more complicated and confusing if mathematics did not exist. We need mathematics to keep track and compare our records. Companies use mathematics to find out if they are losing money or making money. In one way or another, we use mathematics so much that sometimes we do not even realize it.

To begin with, students just do not care and understand mathematics. "A common belief is that you do not need mathematics," says Katie in my math class. Many students have never been introduced to why they need mathematics. My history teacher thinks that, "Students think that if mathematics is not useful to them, then why bother learning it?" Many times, the material that teachers teach is not always understood. Students who do not care about mathematics will not bother to ask questions. Students like these are the ones who keep bringing our success rates down on standardized tests. John, one of the students in my math class believes that, "Students' minds are flooded with false assumptions. For example, they might think that they should do well in math without having to do the work required." An article on mprnews.com stated that, "The United States do not encourage their students enough to do well in mathematics." Students are not motivated to do well because no one is pushing them to do well. To sum it all up, students mainly are not interested in mathematics because they do not understand it and find it useless.

My second reason has to do with the parents. According to an article on foxct.com, "Parents who do not like mathematics do not teach their children why to like mathematics." Due to that, many students will not have the same opportunities in life as students who understand mathematics. Studies show that Whites and Asians are likely to outperform African Americans and Hispanics. Part of this goes back to their parents. Asian and White parents culturally educate their students more regarding why mathematics is important. Many Hispanic and African American families do not do that. Those students who have that support from their parents are expected to do well. This family support helps certain ethnic groups succeed at higher rates. If a parent does not push their child to do well, the child will not know better.

Finally yet importantly, my final reason why students hate mathematics and do poorly on tests is the way they learn math. Students rely on calculators and technology to do the mathematics for them. Students do not understand how they got the answer; they just know that they got the answer. This is not helping them to actually understand the material. I read in an article posted on usatoday.com, "This plays a role on why students fall behind in math classes". Once students have a hard time catching up, they tend to lose interest on the subject. Students then do not understand the material to the best of their ability. Technology may provide a quick fix, but relying on it will not teach them how to solve the problem. When a student is taking a standardized test, the technology is not there or allowed to help them solve the problems. Without calculators, students are lost and confused! When taking a standardized test, it is important to understand the material fully because you need to know how to do it and do it fast. Normally, most standardized tests are timed. If you do not know the material, you waste time. This causes students to do poorly on tests. Part of this can be another reason why students do not like mathematics. Students feel like if they are not good at mathematics, then mathematics is not meant for them.

My recommendation to help students understand and enjoy math is to explain why we learn the subject. Schools have to prove why math is needed; provide students with facts and situations when mathematics is helpful. Schools need to show their students the difference between people who deal with math compared to those who are not involved with mathematics.

Schools also need to do a better job on providing an inspirational learning environment. Schools need to try their best to put students who want to learn mathematics with other students who want to learn mathematics. Get rid of any distractions for those students who truly want to learn mathematics. I feel like this can help improve the apathy towards mathematics.

I recommend parents to teach their children about mathematics by teaching them facts of life. Every child will grow up and need to learn how to survive. Mathematics can help children budget themselves, pay bills, and save money. Who would not want to save money? Parents should also let their children know of the numerous opportunities that are available for those who understand mathematics. There are better paying jobs for those who know and understand mathematics well.

My last recommendation to help students avoid using technology for mathematics is to teach mathematics the old fashion way. Make students write down formulas and make students solve equations on a piece of paper. This will help the student to actually see the work that has been put into solving a problem. Seeing the work put into a mathematic problem helps students understand why a step was taken to solve a problem. Teachers and parents can also use relatable situations to teach mathematics. This will help remember certain things.

I have given you the above reason to draw a better image on why students have apathy towards math. Some of those reasons even play a role in why so many students perform low on standardized mathematics tests. If we can work on changing those reasons to help improve our students' apathy and scores, life could be so much different in the United States. Americans would have better-paid jobs and would for once, be able to compete against Asian countries.

Mathematics can truly help you or hurt you, depending on the way you look or feel about it. As long as you love and understand mathematics, schooling will be much easier for you. If mathematics frustrates you and forces you to dislike it, schooling will be much harder for you. You must choose. Just remember, mathematics is an amazing tool. Knowing mathematics, and being thankful for what it can do for all of us, can take you a long way. Mathematics will continue to be needed and used for years to come.

Dr. Lourdes Ferrer

Juanmanuel Vizcarra

Hello fellow reader, my name is Juanmanuel Vizcarra. I am a Latin American and at this point of life, I have aged 17 years. The majority of Americans believe that the Hispanic community is the laziest of all communities and that statement was true because it reflected my actions in school. That was true until I saw the importance of math and how it is applies in everyday life. Now I am not here to ramble on about my life. I am here to present to you the reasons behind students' apathy towards mathematics and how this reflects in their low performance on standardized tests.

Among the top mathematicians, there has been no consensus on whether mathematics is an art or a science. However, I firmly believe that whether it is an art or a science, math is something we must learn how to excel in. No matter how much one tries to run away from mathematics, it is all around you, from the size of your favorite pair of jeans to the technology you offer your time and life to. As the father of modern physics, Galileo Galilei, once said, "The universe cannot be read until we have learned the language and become familiar with the characters in which it is written, the mathematical language. These letters are triangles, circles and other geometrical figures, without which mean it is humanly impossible to comprehend a single word."

The first reason for students' low performance in standardized test is that we as a society do not push our kids hard enough. Long ago, we lead the world in math and science. Now, other countries are beating our country in both math and science. Their children get homework every night, teachers expect students to complete their homework, and parents respect the teachers' decision expect so. Here in the United States, the students berate the fact that there is such a thing as homework. The same students that loathe the idea of homework are the same ones that do not see themselves as earning the grade; rather they believe that the teacher is giving it to them.

Even though that children are first exposed to math at the age of five, why not help them understand the process to solve simple math problems? Currently we are not really helping our kids learn how to apply math to daily life so that they are able to see the usefulness of mathematics. It is almost as if we reinvented the wheel and our reinvention was more of a square wheel than a round one.

Our kids, nowadays, do not see themselves as earning a grade. But why? Well, it is because parents raise children giving them everything they want. It is noble in intent but in practice produces children who grow expecting everything from everyone else. In countries such as Europe, Asia, India, almost anywhere besides the US, the child self-advocates, they take responsibility. These students know that they have to earn the grade and that a simple phone call from their mom will not belittle the teachers' claim. "Here in the United States, if a parent calls and complains enough about a problem, this problem will be solved," said Jaime Piper, a physics teacher. If this absurdity continues, students being able to overrule their teachers, there will be no American doctors, no American engineers, no American architects. American companies will have to go overseas to find better prospects.

The third reason for students' apathy is the amount of thinking or mental process that it takes to solve a math problem or produce an answer. Solving math problems takes time! Students must understand the process; but if the process does not click right away, they automatically believe that they are not good and stop putting any more effort. Michael Llorens, a statistics teacher said to me, "A student's thought process while asked to answer a question is something like, 'My teacher just showed me step by step the process. If I do not know the answer, then I will look like an idiot.' This kind of thinking makes students give up rather than try to figure out the answer." Students fear more trying not to look dumb that they forget that questioning a teacher's action will help them understand the process of solving, for example, an equation.

The best way for students to improve their education is to ask questions. For example, when you and a couple friends are unsure on how to solve an equation, you can all raise your hands simultaneously. The teacher will have to stop to find out, "What is it that the students are not understanding? Another great way to improve is by getting some individual help from a teacher or a tutor; tutoring will usually take place before or after school. If you are unable to stop your teacher and are unable to get any individual help from someone, push your school to start a homework help club.

The second way to improve students' performance in math has to do with parents. Parents must push their children to strive for big goals. This will spark a sense of maturity and self-growth. Parents who sit by their children while they are doing their homework and try to help them solve the math problems, make their children feel that their parents really care about their education. Children want fulfill their parents' wishes just to see them happy.

The third way to improve a students' education is by simply starting the learning process earlier. The earlier students expose themselves to a new topic, the more experience they gain. Students learn very well at a young age because of the way the brain develops. As a child, I never fully understood how to completely do my multiplications or why I should do them. Now that I am a senior in high school, I see that everything that I learned when I was younger applies to what I do now in my classes.

I believe that math exist in every aspect of the universe, that there is not one single item in existence that does not require or follow a math rule. Leonardo Da Vinci once said, "No knowledge can be certain, if it is not based upon mathematics." We need to teach children the importance of mathematics. If we do not do that, just imagine the opportunities that they will miss. I leave you with this one final question, "What will you do to improve students' ability to comprehend high-level mathematics?"

Dr. Lourdes Ferrer

Laura Serna

In a matter of seconds after takeoff, America's sends its first manned rocket into outer space. I was not there! However, I can almost hear the American people's excitement and feel their happiness bursting out of history textbooks. It was one of the many accomplishments of our nation, and without math, we could have never achieved such a great accomplishment. My name is Laura Serna. I am 16 years old student who attends West Aurora High School. I am writing this paper so we can fix America and feel the excitement that we once felt but with our own dreams. Students are developing a hatred towards math and are scoring low on standardized tests because of bad teachers who do not care, the social acceptance to hate math, and simply because they cannot understand it.

Math is the science that deals with the logic of shape, quantity and arrangement. However, the definition puts me to sleep. Math is all around us, in all the stuff we do, in our clothes, in our phones, TVs, etc., Math is used for everything! It is quite beautiful actually, you know, mainly because it is the same in every language. Math connects us with different parts of the world because it is a universal language. One might think, "When are we ever going to use the Pythagorean Theorem?" or "I don't need to know this." Nevertheless, math is useful and you will need it if you expect to contribute to society in a meaningful way. Math makes our nation stronger. Math is important to create skyscrapers as tall as our dreams. However, sadly, my generation does not understand this. It is time we wake up because eventually, we will have shoes to fill in and it is time we fix our thoughts feelings regarding math.

To begin with, students hate math and are most likely to score low on standardized tests because they simply do not understand mathematics. I talked to a student who had overcome his ADHD. When this student was in middle school, the school thought it was best to simply put him in Special Ed. After a few years, he learned to control his flaw. This student was no longer struggling to concentrate. Therefore, when he got to high school he was put in regular classes. He struggled because in middle school he hardly knew how to do basic algebra! Students are being put into regular classes without a proper foundation, which leads to failure. They cannot be expected to do something they have not even learned. Students who have not learned the minimum are prone to develop hatred towards math and get low scores on standardized tests.

Secondly, I found that students hate math simply because they do not have good teachers. An angry student who

I talked to said, "She just tells us the answers to our past homework, and then gives us our new homework. She doesn't even explain why or how she got the answers!" The student also began to say that she was too afraid to bother the teacher by asking for help because she was always so busy on her laptop. Students who do not have good teachers who care lose interest in math and fall behind.

I also talked to a student who told me his class was "a jungle." When I asked him what he meant, he said that his class never respected the teacher and that the teacher spent 99% of class time "babysitting" students instead of teaching. He had no control whatsoever and basically was a pushover. This is also the students fault. In no way it "ok" or "cool" to disrespect the teacher! The teacher is there for students and they are a huge resource. If teachers are there to help students, why should students treat them with disrespect? On the other hand, it is also the teacher's fault. It is unfair for the students who actually want to learn to sit in class with students who are being disruptive.

Lastly, I came to the realization that students hate math because it has become socially acceptable to be bad at it. I spoke to many students who told me that they were placed in lower classes. This is because in middle school we take a placement test to decide which classes we are going to take in high school. Most students skim through this test because they do not care and are "too young to care." If students score low, they are enrolled in classes where they are a slower pace and spend more time on material they should had learned in 8th grade. They are treated like little babies. Students do not work hard on these placement tests and do not show their true potential. Instead of pushing their limits, they take the easy way out! Rather than lowering our standards, we should raise them! Our society teaches students that it is ok to perform poorly in math. Students think that it is fine to not try to understand math. Students hate math because it is socially acceptance to feel that way.

Our country cannot go on with students hating math. Firstly, I recommend, so we can fix our broken generation, to teach students how important math is. We should do this at an earlier age. By the time our students realize how important mathematics is, it is way too late. If parents start teaching addition and subtraction as early as three or four, then the teachers can move on to bigger things like multiplication and division. Hopefully, if this works, then children can learn algebra as early as 2nd grade! However, students really have to want this; so we need to teach them how important math is. Otherwise, they will go on in life thinking that math is useless and that people do not really need it. These students need to understand that one day they will be running our country.

My second recommendation is to fix our broken teaching system. Teachers are teaching students to memorize equations and memorize theories. Most of the students I talked to do not even know why they are using an equation or when to use it! Teachers need to apply math to real life situations. Students are just memorizing things that they do not fully understand. We should test application not just memorization. If we go on teaching like this, our future generations will not have the vision to see how math can shape their careers.

Lastly, I recommend that we get help from the government. By this, I mean to increase teachers' pay to incentivize more talented individuals to join the teaching profession. They must fund schools appropriately to set this nation up for success. How is it possible that the government can provide funding for guns to fight wars but cannot provide the money to buy an air conditioning unit for a high school? During the summer, my school had to cancel school days. It was too hot to teach. My school, in some parts of the building, does not have air conditioning. It is ridiculous when our education has to be stopped, when it could be so easily be fixed. I also think our government should assist students who have to work to provide for their families. You never know if the cure for cancer is in the brain of a 15-year-old boy who cannot go to school because he has to work to take care of his family. If they are smart and really want an education, then money should never be a problem.

Students hate math because of bad teachers who do not care, it is socially acceptance to hate it, or simply because they do not understand the subject. The United States cannot compete in a global economy if our students hate math and science. We cannot go on being consumers of other countries' ideas and discoveries. We have the opportunity to have our own "space race," but with own new ideas. If we fix this, there is no telling what innovations we will see in the future. The future starts in the classroom. Let us make a better tomorrow for all of us. "Unless someone like you cares a whole awful lot, nothing is going to get better. It's not" – Dr. Seuss.

Lezly Castellanos

It is my last year of high school, but it is not my last year sitting in a math class. Since I was a child, I have always enjoyed math. My friends always say that I am weird, but that is okay. Throughout the years, I have witnessed many students state say that they hate math or that they simply just do not get it. I have always asked myself why students hate math if it so essential in daily life. I made it my task to venture and discover the reasons behind students' hatred towards mathematics. After conducting a series of interviews and research online, I found out that the three greatest reasons for high school students' apathy towards mathematics and low performance on standardized tests are that students might not think that math is important, it is culturally acceptable to hate math, and some math teachers rush through the content.

Many people ask themselves, "What is math and why is it so important? Before I share with you my findings, allow me to explain what math really is. Describing math can be somewhat challenging because it covers so many things. Math is the study of shape, quantity, structure and arrangements using steps, rules and symbols. Even when we do not feel like we are using math, we probably are. When people cook, workout, draw, travel or even when they go shopping, they are using math. Math is essential to our life for many reasons. Without math, money would not really matter. You might be asking yourself "why?" Well, if you have money, but do not know how to manage it, then it is not worth anything. Math will always be present even when we are not able to see it.

The first reason for students' apathy towards mathematics and low performance on standardized tests is that students do not believe that math is important. Many times math teachers are asked, "Why do I need to learn this?" "How am I supposed to use this in life?" or "When is this ever going to be helpful?" For example, last month while we were learning the slope-intercept form of a linear equation, Nicole asked the teacher, "What am I ever going to need this for?" We are young and therefore we have not lived life. In comparison, our teachers are much older and wiser. They have experienced life and had to learn many things. They know that we might not see the importance of learning it now, but they know that it is going to be useful later on. At this age, we are not really sure about what we want to be in life, or what college degree to pursue in college. Students cannot see beyond the day-to-day basis. Who knows? We might end up being a surveyor or an architect that needs to understand the slope-intercept form of a linear equation.

The second reason for students' apathy towards mathematics and low performance on standardized tests is the fact that it is culturally acceptable to hate math. In today's society, hating math is something that is viewed as "cool" among high school students. Many adults say, "I was bad at math in high school," therefore, many students repeat this phrase and believe it. Students then make this as an excuse to not try to do better in their math classes. They say, "My dad was bad in math and so am I." My question is, "Are they really bad at math or are they just repeating what they heard from their parents? On the other hand, being good and liking math puts out an image of being a nerd and being a nerd is not "cool."

The third reason for students' apathy towards mathematics and low performance on standardized tests is the fact that some math teachers rush through the content. Once the bell rings, every math teacher is on a mission. They have to do attendance, teach a new lesson, go over homework, and answer any question - all in about 45 minutes! While students are still taking notes, the teacher already moved on to a different subject. At this point, many students are completely lost. Not all students work and comprehend everything at the same pace. Some may need a little more time, while others catch on quickly. Therefore, students need to ask questions; but nobody does. You may be asking yourself, "Why is it that no one asks questions if no one understands the lesson?" Well, students are afraid to be perceived by their peers as dumb or stupid for asking a question. They feel like everyone understands the material except for them. This leads to students not learning the material and not performing as well as they should or could.

The first thing students, teachers and families can do to help raise students' interest and performance is to work together. When family members work together along with teachers, showing that they care about them, students are encouraged to try harder. When students notice that their parents are taking interest in their education, it makes them feel like they matter and are important. They receive that little push that they might be lacking to succeed in school. Families need to support students at home and encourage them to do better. Family support combine with teacher hard work is what all students need to better their performance in math.

The second recommendation I have for students, teachers, and the community is to provide some type of reward. For example, if the school, or any other institution, rewarded high performance in math, then students would try to do better. Teens have some type of chain reaction on each other. When someone starts doing something that is rewarded, everyone follows whatever he or she is doing. If our schools or our community rewarded students who achieved high performance in math throughout the year in math or on standardized tests, then students would be motivated to also improve. For many students, seeing their peers excel in math is a proof that they can also improve. This could cause a positive chain reaction amongst teenage students.

My third recommendation for students, teachers and schools is to implement better teaching practices. If teachers allow students to participate more in the process of learning, then students can gain a greater understanding of the material being taught in class. In addition, if teachers build stronger relationships with their students, then students could trust their teachers and dare to participate in class. This can lead to students feeling comfortable with asking questions, especially when do not understand, without feeling like they will be judged by their fellow classmates or even their very own teachers.

In Conclusion, there are many reasons behind students' apathy towards mathematics and low performance in standardized tests. Students do not believe math is important; it is also culturally acceptable to hate math; and, some math teachers rush through the content. There are also many ways to help our teenage population understand the importance of math and increase their performance in the subject as well. It is going to take significant effort from not only the students, but also our schools, community and our very own families. I

Dr. Lourdes Ferrer

believe that working together as one could bring great encouragement to our students and hence increase their overall performance.

Lourdes Serrano

"It's too hard!" "I don't understand it!" "When will I ever use it?" These are just some of the many excuses students love to use when it comes to math or any subject that requires a lot of work. After conducting a series of interviews and researching online, I have discovered that the greatest reasons for high school students' apathy towards mathematics and low performance on standardized tests are - the lack of parental participation in their lives; the unfair advantages that some students have over others; and the way the entire education system works.

Children require the attention of a parental figure throughout their lives until the age of 18, when in the United States they are considered adults. However, this is not always the case. It has been proven that parents who attend school events, such as parent-teacher conferences or simple sport games, have a big and positive impact on their children's academic lives. Oppositely, parents who work all day and barely have time to check on their schoolwork, have little to no impact in their children's academic lives. Those children are pretty much on their own. However, some of these families have no other choice but to work all day to put food in their children's mouths. In an interview with a high school student, she mentioned that sometimes students have to worry about children other than themselves. They have to take care of their younger siblings and play mommy or daddy when parents are not around. In her story, she explained to me how every day she has to wake up early, make breakfast for her little brother and get him ready for school. She would use whatever time she has left to take care of herself and get ready for her long day ahead. Some of these kids cannot do their best in school because their minds are not completely focused on their schoolwork. Then, after school, they have to go home and play adult again. In no way I am criticizing parents. I am simply explaining the kind of life many students have. In another interview with a teacher, she explained how as a child, she had to wake up and go to the YMCA where she could she could sleep for an hour and then walk to school. After school, she would walk back to the YMCA and spend the rest of the day there until her mom came back from work to pick her up. Parents who do their best to care for their children see long-term benefits. Parents who supervise their children's schoolwork and push for their best are most likely the parents who get to attend their children's graduation and watch them walk up the steps to receive their diploma.

This brings me to the topic of the unfair advantage some children have over others. For example, the Asian population are stereotyped as high achievers; however, we all know that it is not a lie or a mystery. Malcolm Gladwell, author of the book *Outliers,* goes on to talk about why this is true. He explains that it has to do with their language. According to Gladwell, there is a connection between the time it takes to pronounce or speak something (such as a number) and the memory span of the reader. In their language, they can speak numbers faster than Americans can. This allows them to memorize more numbers at a much younger age. By the age of four, most American children can only count up to 15 while Asian kids can go up to 40. American kids can count up to 40 when they are usually five years old. If we continue with this topic about Asians, we will see that they not only are faster, but they also start learning at a younger age. They prepare for a class before they actually take it and might do it for a different reason. Most of their hard work is done for the sake of honoring their families. In an interview with a 21 year old, an interesting point came up. According to him, "Asians that come to the United States are not yet fully committed to our culture; instead, they keep their studious culture and pass it on to generations." Those students who, like the Asians, are able to achieve bigger stats in education are separated from the rest of the student population. They receive special opportunities that lead to even greater success. In other words, only the best get the best.

Sociologists call this "accumulative advantage." Despite that disadvantage, in an article titled, "Why America Needs Nerds," we take a look at our country and realize that the thing we most praise is sports. Our children are ashamed of admitting they are math geniuses. Why? They fear being picked on and called "nerd." We live in a country where a big achievement is the ability to throw a ball instead of the ability to solve a math problem. These nerds have no voice.

America needs to wake up! Soon, we will no longer be the leading country in the world. It is a shame that this apathy towards math reigns in our society today. It is a huge disadvantage for our children who soon might only be good at kicking a ball instead of finding the cure for cancer.

When students hear the word "test," they freak out and imagine the worst. Their minds are pressured and they are forced to work under stress. When interviewing an older man, he jokingly said, "Tests are the reason every teenager breaks out." He goes on to explain how nowadays, "Studying is not enforced at home because home is not providing a studious environment. Technology has taken over and kids are more focused on what Amanda Bynes did than their algebra homework."

Another teacher expressed that the reason why students test so low is that testing requires memorization skills. Asians do better because they memorize more. In her own words, "Some people are not as good in math as others." My questions is, "How can we determine who is a genius when we are judged based on speed and not understanding? Ron Maggiano, who won two awards (the *Disney Teacher Award* and the *American Historical Association's Beveridge Family Teaching Prize*), retired from his job as a high school teacher because he could no longer be part of a testing regimen. He believes that so much testing is suffocating creativity and innovation in the classroom. In his own words, "We are not really educating our students anymore. We are merely teaching them how to pass a test. This is wrong. Period." Thus, we are obsessed we passing not understanding. When talking to a student, she said, "It was a couple days before finals when I started to freak out. I knew I was struggling with chemistry; but I just had to pass that class! I began to stress myself out, and the next thing I knew, I was laying on a hospital bed hooked up to an IV. I passed out due to so much stress." If you give a student a pencil with a piece of paper and enough time, then you can expect a Shakespeare novel. If students do not have enough time, the result could be a paper with chicken scratches towards the end because of how much they hurry in the process. In a high school English class, a teacher welcomed his student by playing soft nature music the first half of the class and asked them to just relax and focus on their heartbeats. Then the teacher took them out to a courtyard to absorb the beauty of it and write whatever they freely wanted. His students then came back to the classroom and read what they had inscribed. Many were surprised by their striking words. It is because students work better in comfortable and calmer environment than in a room filled with a stifling orchestra and a ticking clock.

Students hate math because they know that some students are just better at it than others are. They feel the pressure to do better in order to pass a test; but at the end, they are ashamed of their lack of knowledge. Moreover, most of them do not have an extra help or a person to boost them up and encourage them to keep moving forward. It is no wonder that in today's society students hate math more than any other subject. When will America realize that our success depends on our ability to teach our young the fundamentals of math? As a high school student, I am unashamed to admit that I am a nerd. This world cannot function without us! True success can only come from hard work and knowledge.

Melany Carrillo

Who am I? The question is very simple, yet complex. Although I am just 16, I recognize I am a blessed Latina Dreamer who is honored to be one of the writers of this book. My name is Melany Carrillo, a junior at West Aurora High School writing to you with the purpose of addressing all the different factors that contribute to students' apathy towards mathematics and low performance in standardized tests.

To begin with, what is math? Math can be perceived as an alien language that is neither pertinent nor related to anything in our world. Like any other foreign language, it must be understood before spoken. Math is life. You may or may not find it interesting; but one thing is true - you must know the basics of mathematics in order to survive in the world. We use math all the time in our daily lives, whether measuring ingredients, calculating the gas money we for a road trip or finding out how much money we need to pay our bills. Without acknowledging the importance of math, most students believe math is useless; therefore, have no concern towards it. After conducting a series of interviews and researching online, I found out that the three greatest reasons for high school students' apathy towards mathematics and low performance on standardized tests are stereotypes, the school teaching system, and students' lack of willpower to think.

We all try to avoid stereotypes; but they are just inevitable! I have seen how they hurt people and it is depressing to see how students fall for senseless stereotypes. A famous stereotype known by everyone is, "Math is hard." I partially agree, math can be hard but only if you have that negative attitude towards trying it. Moreover, everyone has stereotypes, whether you are black, Asian or white. As a Latina, I fall under the category of indolent, unintelligent and mindless but yet a hard working agrarian. It is beyond ridiculous, not only because they do not pertain to every Hispanic person but also because most of my Hispanic peers seem to have fallen for it. Because of this stereotype, many of my peers do not even try. To them, "What's the point?"

Although this might be much like a self-confidence issue, parent involvement and home environment has a lot do with it. My parents have always been supportive and persistent throughout my life. They are willing to do anything to help me successful. I am aware that not everyone has that motivation or healthy home environment to rely on. I remember when I was a freshmen taking Algebra 1. There was a guy sitting in front of me who would constantly fall asleep in class and never really paid attention. When he was awake, he would yap that what the teacher was teaching was useless and asked the students around him, "How is this useful in life?" I asked him, "Don't you care about your future?" He confidently said, "When I'm done with high school, I'm going to open a car workshop and be a mechanic! I don't need this." Dumbfounded by the way he thought, in my head, I questioned myself, "Does he know that he needs to understand gear ratios, volumes and tolerances?" When the teacher asked the class whose parents were coming to the parent-teacher conferences, he answered aloud to himself, "My parents don't care!" My question is, "Why would an ignorant kid try to well in math when his parents do not even care about his grades?

Under those circumstances, another very important contributor to students' apathy towards mathematics and low performance on standardized tests is the entire teaching system. Being a math teacher means being able to teach the students and get them to actually learn and remember the material. Every student learns at a different pace. Some students instantly comprehend the lesson while others need the teacher to slow down or provide more opportunities to practice what they learned. If so, students are to make time after school to stay for extra help; however, this can be a problem for those who may, or may not, have transportation back home. According to one of my math teachers, "We so badly want to slow down but we are not allowed to. We have to teach a certain amount of curriculum before you take the test. As much as we would love to slow down, we are told we can't." If teachers cannot slow down to avoid having students fall behind and students cannot find a way of getting extra help, then there is no change they can get good grades. On the other hand, my physics teacher believes, "No matter what level you teach at, it's always the level before you, the one who screwed up. It can be that what is holding students back in a physics class is not knowing how to rearrange an equation to solve for the variable. In her own words, "You should had learned that stuff when you took Algebra 1, which a lot of you people took during your first year in high school. Now I have you as a junior and still struggling with simple equations." This teacher believes that, "There has to be a better process for making sure that students are ready to move on to the next level." The problem here is that students are passing because teachers cannot fail them. The following year they start already behind, which makes things more difficult for both the student and the new teacher. Math is easy to fall behind but hard to catch up! In my opinion, students should be aware that this is upon them mostly. Nevertheless, if students cannot get support the need, considering both situations, who is really losing here?

Finally yet importantly, the leading reason why students have apathy towards mathematics and perform low on standardized tests is the students' lack of willpower to think. As my fellow friend said, "Math is not like a history class or another class where it's just about memorizing something, all you have to do is spit it out on a test." Math involves multi-step problems that forces students to really think through the solving process. Students need to remember, think and produce an answer to a problem; and all that is a lot of work.

Math is not meant for you to hate it but to help you improve your problem solving skills. The beauty of math is that there is never just one way of solving a problem. In spite of giving students an advantage to learn different ways of solving a problem, some students lack willpower. Laziness causes students to not even try to solve a problem and just give up when they do not know what to do next. Agreeing with my teacher, "Students now are used to having instant gratification. If something takes them longer than just a couple of minutes, they give up. If they have to think a little more than usual or harder than normal, they just give up. They do not want to do it. I think that they are not used to struggling and not used to thinking. Even in video games, if they are having a hard time they find a cheap code somewhere to make it through the game and not die. They will not just play and play until they figure it out. They will ask somebody or find a way around to pass add move to the next level." Consequently, their idleness and lack of determination will only decrease their problem-solving skills and intelligence.

Like any problem, there is always a solution. The first thing teachers and parents can do to improve student's apathy towards mathematics and low performances on standardized tests is to change their approach from reactive to proactive. Parents and teachers ought to try to get students interested in math and emphasize its importance at an early age. Most of my teachers think that schools should facilitate big conferences or meetings to talk about the importance of mathematics and how math proficiency can lead to good colleges and well-paid jobs. This can very well change young students' attitudes towards math.

Furthermore, schools can help improve students' apathy and performances by providing more support. Although students can get help at ACC for math or a math study hall, according to one of my teachers, "I think kids would like help but are reluctant to give up what little social time they have in the school day. Like anyone else, they need some downtime during the school day. A student who struggles in math is not going to spend that 25-minute study hall time getting help with math." That is why I believe that I think that schools can provide an after school activity bus so kids can stay after school to get that extra help. That would get more kids to stay after school. Students and I would greatly appreciate this because it would give us easy extra help. It would also help students' willpower; that way they can take charge of their responsibility to learn the material on their own.

Above all, schools can help improve students' apathy and low performances in math by creating a new teaching system. I, being a student, believe it is completely unfair that teachers have no choice but to rush students to learn an abundant amount of information. This rushing, not only affects students' learning outcomes, but also their performance on high stake standardized tests.

Incisively enough, it is clear that there are many factors that contribute to students' apathy towards math and low performance on standardized tests. The most common are people's negative stereotypes, parents' lack of involvement, teaching system that do not work and students' lack of willpower to think. Deprecating the fact that students may remain poorly educated because of a teaching system that does not work, in my opinion, it all comes down to the students. The students' levity towards math can mostly be blamed on themselves. I believe that if you want to succeed, you will succeed. Like any other goal, academic success will require determination and arduous effort to defeat obstacles and overcome challenges. At the end, this is all about you.

Dr. Lourdes Ferrer

Pablo Melendez

A great man once said, "Mathematics is the most beautiful and most powerful creation of the human spirit." That man was an ingenious mathematician named Stefan Banach. To the judging eye of many, those words of beauty will seem like a scaled lie of some sort. In all honesty, if you were to show that quote to me a couple of years ago, I would most likely disagreed. Then again, I never saw the true essence of mathematics. Math is like a puzzle. There are all these twist and turns. Piece by piece, it all fuses into one at a certain point. Once it is all done, you feel a surge of joy for acquiring new knowledge. That is the power of math! It empowers the person with knowledge on everything that surrounds him. For example, an engineer of any sort converts math to matter by creating such things as buildings, cars, bridges, and so much more. Math is so vast that it seems to have no boundaries. Unfortunately, so many people's love for math deteriorates because they have been taught to not view it as important.

Progressing through my research, I realized one crucial factor in the development of any human being, their brain. It is not until the age of twenty-five that the brain is fully developed. The amygdala, the part of the brain that deals with emotions, rationalizes many of our common life decisions. One big reason why students dislike math is that they have moments in their life where they struggle with math. This goes hand in hand with the amygdala. As the student begins to struggle with math, their amygdala takes over and puts thoughts in their head that makes them dislike mathematics. Because of this, students remain hating the idea of learning math. Many other factors can alter this effect. For example, if teachers do not try to help students, then they will remain hating math. This is why so many students hate math. Not only their brains, but their teachers also play a big part in this. Their minds are clouded by emotions that crowd their minds when it comes to solving math problems. If teachers add even more stress and trouble, then students will just shut down and fail.

The ACT, otherwise known as a junior's worst enemy, is an instrumental part in students' careers. It decides many of the students' short-term goals during their last year in high school. In addition, the stress of doing well in school and keeping up their GPA puts a lot of pressure on students. Both of these lead to another reason why students hate math.

Many students feel like, they cannot take it anymore! They feel that they are forced to sacrifice so much time to perform well in all their classes. My physics teacher, Mr. Stern, had some very interesting opinions on this subject. For example, if students have ferocious doubts in their minds about themselves, then they will find it harder to enhance their math skills and could quite possibly hate math permanently. If students set themselves into believing that they are not good at math, then they will hold on to that lie and never see the importance of mathematics.

The brain is the engine of the entire human body. Everything that goes on in our body is carried out or controlled by some part in our brain. It is something truly beautiful. The brain is composed of an array of neurons that intertwine with one another to form these systems that send messages to the whole body. The left hemisphere of our brain controls the logical side of life, such as math and language. One big reason why students have problems with math is that students do not find the importance in math. The reason why these students do not feel the need to prioritize math and do not see the need for math is that they do not develop the link that creates love, which could significantly increase their performance.

One example of the effects of the brain is the popular condition called math anxiety. This phenomenon affects children at any age by not allowing them to properly analyze the puzzling part of math. This not only affects learning but attitude, which leads to decreased potential. Today, problems like these are what cause students to not prioritize math. It is not because they do not try, rather than, it is the fact that these students have not been able to see and experience the importance of math. That link is not in their brains.

When the time comes, no one should just sit and wait. It is time for everyone to find a solution. A way to pitch in and help is changing this biased and negative belief regarding math. The point is that, if students are mentally wired to think that they are not good at math, they will stay thinking they are not good enough at math. Mrs. Cirrincione, my Algebra 2 teacher, is more than correct when she said, "We can change this by stop accepting math intolerance from students. It is wrong to believe that they are incapable of performing well at math."

Those that can pitch in to help students are parents and teachers. Teachers could do so much more than just their "job," even if it means going an extra mile to help students out. Schools can improve students' attitude through ACT practices. Parents can learn how to help their children through parent workshops. Parents can also do what Dr. Ferrer says, "Parents should not push but pull their kids to work harder and become better students." It is her belief that parents should lead by example. They must demonstrate with their life how their children can achieve academic success.

Repeatedly, we encounter situations where students test poorly on sections of the ACT, precisely the math portion, and even with practice, they still perform poorly. Why is this happening? After my interviews, a light flashed above my head. The greatest dilemma with tests like the ACT is not the material tested but the significance of the test. The stress is overwhelming! Trust me, I know. One possible way to minimize this overwhelming stress is to let students now that their ACT scores just show college readiness, not if they are smart enough to enroll in college. If students are unfortunate enough to score poorly on these tests, they could easily be demoralized by the results. If we could address this problem, we could potentially see better results. Stress and hardship would not affect students' performance that much and students would do better.

Looking back at different students' early years, you might notice one gargantuan problem. Many students simply lack the discipline to excel in school. They grow up with lenient parents and easy teachers, making it easy for students to perform below the standard. The problem here is that when students face serious academic challenges, they crack easily with the pressure. One way we can counteract this lack of discipline is by teaching students the importance of routines and structure in their education and how to organize their lives to experience greater academic success. The stronger the "pillars" of their academic structure, the more likely they are to succeed. When you present students with a challenge and they do well, they begin to work harder and become better. Students like to overcome challenges. It makes them feel good about themselves. On the other hand, when you present students with a challenge and they do not perform well, they stop trying. They feel criticized by their peers and if their peers perform well, then they feel like a failure. A close acquaintance of mine, Mr. Zafra, shared with me what I just said. Teachers need to understand how common this is. You cannot expect a seed to sprout without watering it. Give the students the "water" they need to grow on their own. That will give them the opportunity to develop the grit they need to succeed in life. At some point in their live, students will realize that all the hard work they put into learning was totally worth it! Eventually, it will be clear to all students how important it is to be gritty and behave in a responsible manner.

At the end of the day, this research is not about personal gain. It is about learning and comprehending the greatness of math. Its beauty cannot be unmasked for it is true and pure. Mathematics shines a light into the black voids in our minds. Once you truly learn math, it cannot be undone. Your life seems to be a bit clearer when you accept mathematics as a crucial part of your life. In reality, this world demands people who master math and can bend it to their advantage. Careers in medicine, computer software, engineering, to name a few, demand a strong foundation in mathematics. These are precisely the ones in high demand here in the United States and around the world.

Like everything else in life, never give up after the first time you experience failure. Failure teaches humans to stand back up and try even harder. According to Summer Redstone, American businessperson and media magnate, "Success is not built on success. It is built on failure. It is built on frustration. Sometimes it's built on catastrophe."

Dr. Lourdes Ferrer

DR. LOURDES' BIO

Growing up in a disadvantaged family in Puerto Rico, Lourdes soon learned that education was the way out of the poverty cycle. This understanding led her to complete her undergraduate degree in mathematics and begin teaching.

She left Puerto Rico in 1979 to do community development work in Guatemala. She established and directed schools, an orphanage, feeding centers, and clinics. She procured resources for these entities through interaction with non-profit organizations and by obtaining assistance from Guatemalan government officials. Her community education work consisted of educational radio programs and parent education in various venues. Her experience in community development was a catalyst that led Lourdes to choose Research, Evaluation, and Measurement as the focus of her Master's degree.

When she moved to the United States in 1990, she had to overcome enormous financial, linguistic, and cultural barriers to pursue the American Dream. She first worked as a Middle School Bilingual Curriculum Content (BCC) mathematics teacher in Dade County and then as Regular High School mathematics teacher in Palm Beach County.

She went on to complete her Doctoral Degree in Leadership and took a position as a School Improvement and Assessment Specialist for the School District of Palm Beach County. She was responsible for developing and implementing programs that assist schools in their school improvement efforts. These programs included staff development opportunities for teachers and school administrators, assessment literacy presentations as well as speaking at community forums regarding student academic achievement and performance gaps between diverse student populations.

In 2005, Dr. Lourdes left Florida to work as an Education Consultant in DuPage County, Illinois, and other school districts across the nation. Since then she has been analyzing student performance data and conducting qualitative studies to find out from the students', teachers' and parents' perspectives the reasons behind the lack of academic achievement of students on states' accountability tests. For the past eight years, she has developed numerous programs designed to increase the academic achievement of all students and close the stubborn academic achievement gaps between diverse student populations. These programs include state-approved academies for school administrators, staff development opportunities, student motivation presentations and parent empowerment seminars.

Dr. Lourdes' specializes in academic and non-academic issues regarding English Language Learners, Hispanic and African American students. She covers a wide range of topics that include cultural competency, achievement gaps between ethnic groups, parent empowerment, culturally relevant instruction, college and career readiness, math Common Core State Standards and state's accountability testing.

Dr. Lourdes is the author and facilitator of, Navigating the American Educational System (NAES) and In the Driver's Seat, two very popular and dynamic curricular and training programs, designed to help parents navigate the American Education System, monitor their children's education and ensure that their children receive a top-quality education.

She is also the author and facilitator of the Grooming for Excellence Student Leadership academy, a program designed to increase students' college and career readiness, motivate them to pursue STEM-related degrees and graduate college with the least amount of debts.

Dr. Lourdes is the author of the books Hispanic Parental Involvement: Ten Competencies Schools Must Teach Hispanic Parents, Siéntese en la Silla del Conductor: Las Diez Competencias Para Conducir a Sus Hijos al Triunfo Académico and the co-author of Voices: African American and Hispanic Students' Perceptions Regarding the Academic Achievement Gap. Her latest publications, Reactions: A Collection of Hispanic

Dr. Lourdes Ferrer

Student Essays, Reactions: A Collection of African American Student Essays and College Casualties: Twelve Competencies to Avoid Becoming One are different from any other publication because she wrote them in collaboration with high school students.

DEBORAH'S BIO

Deborah Ferrer was born in Guatemala, Central America, a country also known as - the land of the eternal spring. In pursuit of a better life, at the age of four, her family migrated into the United States and established themselves in Florida. According to her mom, "During our first year, Deborah was the one who struggled the most. Going to school made her seriously ill. It made things very difficult for all of us."

After Deborah reached grade-level English proficiency and learned how to navigate the American culture, her mother enrolled her at U.B. Kinsey Elementary School of the Arts, one of the best elementary school in the county. At that early age, Deborah fell in love with the visual arts! She continued her pursuit of a highly specialized education in the arts throughout her middle school years. In 2000, she was admitted to the Alexander W. Dreyfoos School of the Arts, a nationally recognized high school in Palm Beach County. In her own word, "I literately battled to get myself accepted into that school. Hundreds of young artists auditioned and very few were accepted."

As a teenager, Deborah was determined to pursue a college career that required a strong foundation in the visual arts. To reach that goal she took advantage of every opportunity her high school offered. Besides meeting the school's visual arts requirements, she took all types of rigorous academic subjects. To earn some college credits, save some money and time, she enrolled and successfully passed the exams for AP Spanish and AP History.

Although Deborah was raised in home environment where the culture of learning prevailed, she knew that her mother, a single parent of three, was not in a position to cover all the costs of an out-of-state private university. She knew that to be accepted, and be able to finance her college education, she had to have a good GPA and a high ACT score. In her own words, "I was totally focused and I worked really hard!" In 2004, she graduated with a 4.5 GPA and an ACT score of 30. Her hard work paid off! She was one, of only 60 students nationwide, who received a 100,000-dollar scholarship to attend the Cooper Union School of Art, an elite university in New York City. Living in Florida at the time, this awesome news presented several challenges. She was a girl, the youngest of three children, and the first in the family to move thousands of miles away from home to pursue a degree in Fine Arts - something not common in the Hispanic culture.

Deborah soon fell in love with New York; and not long after that, she discovered the world of Architecture, a career that beautifully combines fine arts with applied mathematics. In 2006, she was accepted to the Irwin S. Chanin School of Architecture at the Cooper Union, a five-year degree program, and was the recipient of another 125,000 dollars in scholarships to cover her tuition.

Within those 5 years working towards her Architecture degree, she made another discovery – she had an innate passion for management and administration. She was hired by the Dean of the School of Architecture to manage the school computer studio. She worked as a manager for five years and her responsibilities included - supervising staff, meeting the students' computer needs, providing staff development and increasing the efficiency of the equipment.

In 2008, her sense of adventure, multicultural perspective and high academic performance got her into Ghana, Africa. She received a scholarship to study and build in a small under-developed village, a traditional adobe construction, using both new and old construction techniques. In spite of the challenges that an under-developed community presents, she successfully completed her work with the support of the villagers. Her likeability contracted the attention and love of the people.

In 2010, she earned another scholarship to travel to her home country of Guatemala to complete her college thesis.

Her love for Guatemala, ability to communicate in Spanish and bold spirit opened wide doors to learn from Guatemalan engineers, architects and the community in general, the reasons behind the capital's sink holes. In spite of the government's opposition, she was able to get evidence that these 100 feet deep holes were created not solely by nature, but by leaking pipes of the sewer system, due to lack of maintenance, lax city zoning regulations and building codes. She earned the Cooper Union medal for Leadership and Excellence upon graduation in 2011.

Soon after graduating, she started working as a project manager for a construction firm in Orlando, Florida until 2012. During this year, she was able to see firsthand the strong connection that exists between civil engineers, architects and construction companies. She was able to experience the challenges of building homes that meet the clients' demands, within budgets and in accordance to the city's building codes. In her own words, "That year was worth a life of experience!"

Following her passion for business management, she put her architecture career aside, at least for a while, to accept a position as a Business Manager in a worldwide company specialized in exotic teas. Her responsibilities include hiring and training personnel, scheduling, doing payroll and most of all, meeting the company's financial goals for her ½-million dollar store. Since then, she has twice won a Certificate of

Excellence and been recognized as one of the top ten General Managers in the company.

Ms. Ferrer also operates her own small business called Paper Cut, working as an art consultant, graphic and interior designer and book editor. She is also the co-author of the book, College Casualties: Twelve Competencies to Avoid Becoming One." This book, written for high school students (and their parents) provides readers with strategies to avoid dropping out of college, earning degrees that are not in demand or graduating with surmountable debts. Her goals right now are to - further develop her business skills, pursue a Project Management Certification and later on, earn a Master's in Material Science from MIT.

Proof